You Empowered Strong

Infinite Possibilities in the Power of Y.E.S.

Y.E.S.
You Empowered Strong

Candy Barone

ISBN: 1492816191
ISBN 13: 9781492816195

Y.E.S. Philosophy

You, Empowered Strong, can …

Define your own path
Be an impactful leader
Make a difference every day
Inspire others to dream bigger
Earn the respect you deserve
Define your character
Live your life with passion
Be great & be bold
Dare to try new experiences
Take control of your destiny
Decide to be happy & fulfilled

Table of Contents

Acknowledgments   vii

Introduction   xi

One: The 'Too' Box   1

Two: Finding 'The' Way   11

Three: Where There's a Will and a Way, There Better Be a Why   19

Four: Get Off the Treadmill and Build a New Road   29

Five: The Power and Intention of the Words You Choose   39

Six: Destroy the Noise: Stop 'Should-ing' All Over Yourself   51

Seven: Walk the Talk   61

Eight: Be Coachable *Not* Controllable   69

Nine: Go Big, or Go Bigger … Forget Going Home   77

Ten: Celebrate the Victories & the Failures No Matter How Small   81

Eleven: The 3 'Is: Inspire, Influence, Impact   87

Twelve: You ARE Empowered Strong!   93

About the Author   97

Acknowledgments

Any time you begin to embark upon your life's purpose and truly begin to create magic on the dreams in your heart, you start to realize that your path was paved with so much love, support, and friendship along the way. That definitely was the case as I wrote this book. As everything started to take shape and come together, I found myself reflecting on my own journey and how I arrived at this juncture in my life. As I did, I was filled with such gratitude and love for all those who have impacted me along this journey. I remember the laughs, the struggles, the advice, and the overflowing of support I have been blessed with each and every day. So, as I introduce this book to you, I feel I would be remiss if I didn't take a moment to thank those people who influenced me, helped make this book a reality, and helped shape me in becoming the person I am today.

To Corie Hill, thank you for always having unwavering faith in me and for challenging me to dream bigger. For almost thirty years, you have loved me for who I am, provided me with great insight and truth, been the very best friend I could ever ask for, and have always had my back. For that, and so much more, I am forever grateful and I love you.

To Andrea Nordgren, thank you for being a true friend, a business consultant, and a partner to me in this journey. Your insight, feedback, and assistance have meant so much, and I appreciate all that you continue to share with me, teach me, and hold me accountable to. I am honored that you created the cover design for this book—for you are gifted in so many ways, and I feel blessed that you have shared your talent with me.

To Sharen King, thank you for believing in my ability to lead and giving me the freedom to find my true north and be authentic. Thank you for constantly reminding me that I am a "powerful child of God." I also thank you for being my biggest cheerleader and champion in promoting my talents, letting them shine, and helping me learn which "dog to feed." You have forever left a mark on my life and in my heart.

To Karice Stern, thank you for being a catalyst and reminder to go after only those things that make my "heart dance." You continually demonstrate that there are no boundaries for what one can accomplish in this lifetime, and I continue to admire you for everything you have achieved and continue to achieve.

To Sarah Koenig, thank you for being a "sister" to me and being my balance. From the minute we first met, we seemed to be two puzzle pieces that just fit together. And, as our friendship grew, we definitely learned that "one shoe really can change your life" and make a lasting imprint on how you carry yourself forward.

To Michelle Dhein, Shawna Muren, Claire Myers, Faith Bose, Chris Sutter, Becky Ploeckelman, Lisa Goodpaster, Jessie Waack, Amy Turzai, Yvonne Kennedy-Harris, Candy Ruh, Jen Hulbert, Niki Pettit, Becky Galten, Jen Memken, Heather MacKenzie, Diana Moro-Goane, Lauren Trotnow, Barb Gerrits, Kim Niemi, and Jessica Karis, thank you all for being my "girls", my rocks, and my confidants over the years! Thank you for your kindness, your honesty, and your overflowing generosity of heart. You always have seen me as just *me*. I admire you all so much as you continue to live your life giving so much to others every day, without judgment, and only with compassion. Thank you for all the laughs and tears over the years! Pure of heart and fiercely loyal, you exude a grace and honesty that is truly to be admired.

To Mark Diestlemeier, thank you for always having my back and supporting me whenever I needed a friend with no questions asked. You have been a true friend in every sense of the word, and I consider myself incredibly blessed to have you in my life.

To Rik Akey, thank you for being such an inspiration in leading by example. You exemplify the meaning of "no excuses" and have set the bar for achievement extremely high. I also want to thank you for coaching me during my half-marathon training and for fine-tuning one of my favorite sayings. As you put it so bluntly to me once, for me, it's all about "go big, or go bigger." That moment changed so much for me, and inspired one of the topics I now speak on. So, again, thank you.

To Myra De La Paz, thank you for showing me a new perspective and a more productive way to go after the things I want most without muscling through the pain and agony every time. I thank you most for the patience, acceptance, and self-truth you gave me along the way in our journey together. I love you, girl!

To Kevin Chadwick, thank you for showing me the path to finding my own "decided heart." From our conversation that first time we talked at the conference where we met to our growing friendship now, I feel as if our paths were meant to cross. I greatly admire your leadership, your spirit, and your humility, and someday I hope to be as "big time" as you.

To Kelly Sikes, thank you for being my road warrior and helping me make the move cross-country to live out my dreams. You are a man of great integrity, compassion, and heart, and I am glad we found ourselves in sales training together many, many years ago. You are family to me, and I am so grateful for your friendship.

To my family, thank you for always believing in me, letting me fly my own course and never trying to clip my wings. I love you more than words could ever express. Together, we have gone through many trials and tribulations, so many ups and downs; yet, the journey only has made us stronger. Mom, Chad, and Crystal, you are my heart, my soul, and the very foundation on which I am able to stand and grow. I love you all so much and words cannot begin to express how much you mean to me.

To the Kempfs, the whole lot of you, thank you for being my surrogate family and welcoming me into your circle and family. You have given me so much love and so many memories over the years. You truly adopted me with open arms and into your hearts. I am forever grateful for your kindness, generosity, and friendship, and the endless amounts of laughter and tears we have shared.

To ALL my friends (old and new, and from so many facets of my life), extended family, , advocates, supporters, mentors, coaches, and champions over the years and across the globe, thank you so very much for the lessons you taught me, the grace you have given me, the faith you have in me, and so many laughs, memories, and experiences you shared with me. I am so blessed to have you all in my life, as you have given me such joy and influenced greatly who I am today.

I dedicate this book to each of you, as I cannot thank you enough for playing such significant roles in my life. I am so blessed and filled with gratitude as I think of the role each of you has had in helping me truly become *empowered strong*.

Thank you.

Introduction

"The question isn't who is going to let me; it's who is going to stop me."
– Ayn Rand

Are you ready to repower and recharge your life? To delve deeper into your passions and start living your life to the fullest? Are you looking to create balance in all aspects of your life? Maybe you feel "stuck" or that you are not achieving the results you really want. Maybe you don't know where to start or are trying to find your purpose in your life. Maybe you have been successful, and you keep going, going, going … only to find yourself running in circles or caught on the treadmill of life.

Would you like to do more, be more, and achieve more? What if you could do all that and then some, simply by redirecting the way you currently think, by creating a functional road map that allows for alternate routes? Would you be interested in learning how to better use tools you already have, so that your investment to get more would be minimal, but much more focused?

Wherever you find yourself, look no further … for you, my friend, have arrived at the right stop on your journey. This book is for *you*!! A place where you can start to gain clarity of thought, emotional balance and stability, congruence in your own life, personal and professional development, reflection, confidence, and harmony—not to mention walking away with tools you can use immediately to enhance and refocus your own life.

You Empowered Strong: Infinite Possibilities in the Power of Y.E.S. guides you through an inspired journey that provides conscious awareness, helping you tap into your own resources to empower yourself beyond what you think is possible. This book is designed to address areas where you typically find yourself getting "stuck," help you identify what those barriers might be and how to address them proactively.

In addition, this book will help you understand and clarify your goals, which oftentimes can be limited by your own assumptions, expectations, judgments, or old ways of thinking. I will help you define your goals and bring them into reality by helping you tap into the tools you need to create a clear road map and plan of action to help you achieve your desired outcomes.

You Empowered Strong provides a conduit to enable you to maximize the resources and skills you already possess to help you become "unstuck" and free yourself from some of your existing barriers, your excuses, and current ways of thinking. You may find that this book simply provides a means for you to achieve a greater level of success, or you may find it serves as a means to create greater alignment and congruence with what you say you want and what you are doing every day.

Whatever currently is getting in your way, my book is designed to help you recognize those limiting influences and help you tap into the powerful resources you already possess. This book is structured with the end in mind, and allows us to start with where you are right now. The past cannot be changed and is just that, the past. Let it be what it is—it only serves as a resource from which to learn, and the future has not happened and is still open for design.

So, in order to maximize what you can draw from this book, let's focus on the here-and-now, the present, what you can control and change, and help you build a road map to get everything your heart desires and make your dreams a reality.

The first step will be to identify your goals and understand what you really want in your life. Then, we will need to determine what's getting in your way, slowing you down, or completely sabotaging you from getting what you say you truly want. I will help you understand why now is the time for you to take action.

After that, you will be able to put a game plan together to address those barriers and outline how you can make some changes in your thinking, your beliefs, and your current actions to really get what you want most (personally and professionally).

Finally, I will provide guidelines on how best to use the resources you already possess to build a plan that you can stay focused on and accountable to in order to provide you with ongoing and sustainable success.

As you go through this book, you will see that I start and end each chapter with a quote to help put your mind in the right frame to embrace the learnings I hope you will be able to take with you. I also will share stories of various experiences, drawn both from my own personal life, as well as coaching sessions I have had with clients, to help illustrate the points I want to make.

At the end of each chapter, I give you a "call to action" or exercises as a takeaway so you can start using the tools and thinking in your life right away. Though this book is meant to flow from one chapter to the next, I also designed it in a way to allow you to come back to any specific chapter or point, at any time, without needing to reread the entire book. This book is your tool to help you create and navigate your own road map. It is your guide, and I hope you come back to it often.

So, now, are you ready to get started and to live the life of your dreams and the one you truly deserve? Are you ready to sing the song that's in your heart and yours alone to share with the world? Are you ready to shine your light in the brightest and most magnificent way possible? If so, then let's begin your journey … For *you* are the only thing getting in your own way. Currently, you might be limited by the barriers you have created from what you were told in the past, what you have learned over the years, your prior experiences, your existing beliefs, and the excuses you have been making. Now, is the time to change all that!

Oftentimes, these barriers and learned behaviors play into the negativity and fear you hold within your own thoughts. You currently are holding yourself back by the things you think, speak, and believe. It is time to break free from those barriers and limiting influences and set yourself free once and for all. For your potential is limitless, if you only imagine it so and decide to embrace it fully.

Like the eagle you see on the front cover of this book, this is YOUR time to fly high and soar to new heights. Now is the time to make a commitment to yourself and recognize what you truly deserve. Rise above your excuses and your fears and live your life as an eagle, a visionary who seeks opportunity, great strength, and freedom. Fly strong and empower yourself as the eagle does and own YOUR sky.

Dream it. Build it. Achieve it. Live it. There are infinite possibilities in the power of Y.E.S.

I believe every journey, no matter how difficult, starts with our own faith and beliefs. The road is not always easy, and I know there will be hurdles to overcome. So I ask, during our time together, that you trust yourself, your own capacity for greatness, and this process we are about to embark upon. Have faith in what is different, what challenges you, and enjoy the journey as much as the reward. Find the place where you can quiet down and allow yourself to dream.

For me, I find that I am able to quiet down my mind and heart through prayer, and allow peace to guide me forward. If prayer is not for you, then I challenge you to find your own sense of peace, whether by meditation, relaxation, or whatever else you might do to truly quiet down the noise inside. It is important that you calm down your mind and heart to start the journey of truly embracing and embarking upon change.

In order to focus, gain awareness, and persevere, one must be in a place to receive, learn, and grow. If there is noise and other distractions all around you, this becomes almost impossible to do. So, find your space, and we can truly begin to unleash and unlock your greater potential.

For those who do find prayer gives you that peace, here is a prayer I wrote and use often to help me whenever I feel frustrated or as if my life isn't moving in the direction that I really want, or when I simply need to reset and put myself back in a space to accept the greatness within me.

I have found that I gain so much more control when I truly surrender in my faith, and let go of the need *to* control. I pray, hold onto my faith, and let go of the need to understand the "why" and "how" for everything in my life. I trust that my journey is the one I am meant to be on, and that God only gives me that which I can handle and grow from. Everything happens with purpose and that is *why* enough.

So, I wanted to share my prayer with you, no matter where you are in your journey, as I find these words help me to refocus and breath, whether I am feeling stuck myself (yes, even coaches need to refocus from time to time, as it is human nature to get off course when we lose sight of our own compelling why), or am hurting, simply feel lost, or just need to remind myself to focus from within, and with God, and to be grateful for the blessings and gifts I have received. An *attitude of gratitude* truly is one of the most powerful tools you have to be great.

With that, I hope you find these words, or your own, do the same for you, to help you regain or tap into your faith and set your compass north again. Thank you for entrusting me to help guide you in your journey.

Dear Lord,

Help me find my way. I feel like recently I have gotten off the path I want to be on and the one you intended for me. I have lost some faith along the way to guide me down the path that is truly mine. My heart is open to your love. I want to receive love, believe in love, and be open to love fully without reservation. Not only does this mean love of others, but love of myself as well.

I want to achieve the greatest depths of love through your guidance and accept love from others and for myself. I want to love full out and big, and hope to be able to accept that magnitude of love in return. Help me find my way back. Help me trust in my faith and in your love. Help me to believe in hope again.

In the reflection of your love, I will see the true image of myself, a representation of your perfection. Faith in love, so pure and unyielding, without judgment for the past or apprehension for the future, truly will be the catalyst that sets me free. For the present is the only opportunity to witness the miracles of my soul and to love in all your glory.

Forgiveness and faith also will be key in unlocking the walls I have cemented and the barriers I have built. Forgiveness for myself and of myself will be my biggest challenge, yet my greatest reward. For forgiveness will allow love to flow freely from within my heart.

I also no longer wish for my fears to paralyze me, but instead I ask for your guidance. I humbly ask you to help me find peace and love within myself, and to be courageous in my quest for truth and growth.

For I am a glorious and powerful child of God. I strive to live a more loving, more beautiful, and more harmonious life. I thank you for the amazing gifts you have graciously bestowed upon me. I will embrace these gifts fully and without fear. I know I was created to be great and to sing the song within my heart.

Through this journey, I will start to learn how to abundantly live my life with a greater sense of mission and purpose. I will allow my true self to shine the light that is only mine to give.

With my faith in your grace, I humbly thank you.

Your grateful servant,

Amen.

Let's get started ...

"The two most important days in your life are the day you are born and the day you find out why."
– Mark Twain

one

The 'Too' Box

*"Every child is an artist. The problem is how
to remain an artist once he grows up."*
– Pablo Picasso

For as long back as I can think, people have tried to put me in what I like to refer to as the "too" box. Even as a kid well before preschool, I heard, "Candy is too independent, too stubborn, too vocal, too *whatever*." Then, as I entered preschool and kindergarten, my "too" box started to grow bigger and bigger. I was told I was too creative, too inquisitive, and that I didn't play well by the rules.

I can remember one instance when I was reprimanded in kindergarten for coloring my sky red in a drawing. I remember coloring with pure passion and fervor as I was proud of the masterpiece I was creating. However, I was told that the sky had to be blue, and always should be blue. Everyone knew that the sky should be blue. I, on the other hand, questioned this reasoning as the sunset the night before proved that wrong. The sky wasn't blue at all as the sun was going down. Something didn't seem to make sense to me.

With its magnificent colors of deep red, purple, and orange splashed across the sky, as I saw it the night before, the sky was everything and anything but blue. I didn't understand. I was just trying to re-create what I had seen the night before. I was trying to make my drawing come to life just like the sky was to me. But, again, I was told the sky was to be blue. In that moment, and in many more instances to come later on, it became very clear that if I were to color the sky, and not cause trouble, then it had better be blue.

I remember being angry and feeling defeated in that moment, as I took in the literal meaning of everything when I was a child. I came home upset, frustrated, and confused. I remember crying to my mom as I retold the story. My literal mind fought so hard to understand, as I took everything at face value. I simply couldn't comprehend why I had to "lie" and make my sky blue … when it just wasn't so the night before. I simply couldn't understand why I got in trouble for coloring my sky exactly as I had seen it with my very own eyes and what was still in my memory.

And so, frustrated and confused, the constraints of my "too" box began to expand. I also can look back and remember getting my first report cards in elementary school, and teachers would tell my mom, "Candy is extremely bright, but too inquisitive." Wow, again that didn't make sense to me (and still doesn't really to this day)—I mean, too inquisitive? Hmmm, is that even possible?

And with all those "toos," I struggle with the balance of wanting to please others, play by the rules, and not get in trouble. Yet, I found this so challenging, as I saw things as very 'black-and-white' and wanted to know why things were the way they were, and to know who decided that something was to be. I had my own way of interpreting the world around me, as do many children; yet, these are the boundaries and limitations we put on them and on ourselves all the time.

We fight so hard to have children color "inside the lines" during their development years and in everything they do growing up (e.g., in school, in sports, in all of their outside extracurricular activities) that we cannot understand why it is so difficult for them to then "think outside of the box" as adults. There is this sense of wanting everything and everyone to fit inside a certain framework, or mold, or box that is safe and looks like everyone else, and we lose so much creativity and individuality, as a result—and, to think, we stifle those things only out of fear, limited thinking, and our beliefs.

As an adolescent, I was labeled 'too" all throughout school because I asked a lot of questions and I had a strong sense of self, even back then. When someone would tell me something, I wanted to know *why* and *how*. I wanted to understand where ideas came from, who decided something was to be, and how things worked. I was curious, an explorer of life, hungry for knowledge, someone seeking to experience everything and anything I could wrap my brain around or get my hands on; I had a thirst for answers and expanded thinking.

Though I was a kid, I had a voice, a perspective, an opinion, my own way of seeing things and was voracious for more. For some reason, this made people nervous. It made lots of people nervous, especially the older I got. I fought against those that wanted to put me in a box so hard throughout my life, those who wanted to make me think like everyone else, that I usually felt exhausted, defeated, and angry that I was asked or told to conform so much. It felt as if all my energy at times was in fighting against standards and norms.

The more I felt I had to fight, the more it made me want to be different even more, just so I wouldn't be put into the "too" box any longer. I wanted to challenge, to test, to think, to wonder, to try on, to dream, to understand more, to … well, to learn. And I wanted to be *me*, whoever and whatever that was to be. I didn't want anyone to tell me what that looked like either, who I was *supposed* to be. I wanted to figure that out myself. (Yes, I do have a rather mean, stubborn, and independent streak that is fueled from my core.)

But I found that so many people were afraid of just that, what might be different, what might be strong. So many seem so afraid of what is outside of their accepted, safe box they conform to and, thereby, try to break down anyone who dares to venture outside of it. Because I didn't fit the box in most cases, this seemed to make people even more determined to put me in it, and of course, on the flip side, I fought even harder to stay out of it. They pushed, I fought. I fought, they pushed … and, so forth.

A crazy, endless game of tug-of-war, I assure you. And it was exhausting. Even now, in how I think and process information, I like to challenge myself and what is expected. I find myself to be pretty balanced between both sides of my brain, and people struggled in needing to define whether I was more analytical (the engineer in me) or more creative (the writer and poet in me). For some reason, they struggled and it wasn't acceptable to be both. I had to fit a box! Or so I thought.

Let's pause for a moment and think about how many of our current frameworks oftentimes limit our youth and how they think every day. It has been only recently that schools have started acknowledging there are many different ways children learn and take in information. Some are more visual learners, some auditory, and others use their senses, or are more kinesthetic.

And there are multiple layers from there. Imagine if we only changed our learning to support these different styles versus trying to break them down and do what we always have done. And what's ironic is that children who learn and take in information differently become adults who do the same. We can learn new methods, but our inherent style for accessing and understanding information never leaves us. Wouldn't we be more productive if we played to those strengths versus trying to break them down to fit a box?

OK, I digressed there for a moment, back to the larger point I am trying to make. So, the "too" box was created and kept growing all around me. The more I dared to be true to myself, the more others tried to insist I taper my thinking. Whenever I would ask "why," I would be given the common response, "because." And all this would do was increase my appetite to know more, to dig deeper. "Because why?" I would respond. It became an endless cycle that only got bigger and more intense as I moved throughout my adolescence and into adulthood, and then into my career.

Now, don't get me wrong, I have been and am very successful in my life, my education, and my career. As an overachiever of sorts, and most definitely a strong type A personality, I always have been determined to be on top of my game and strive for achievement. I enjoyed getting praise, promotions, bonuses, and the like for being a top performer. I was easily motivated by these rewards throughout the bulk of my corporate career. I was a perfectionist who learned the rules of the game and was determined to master every domain I played in.

However, as I became more comfortable with my own sense of self, my ability to lead, and my own voice, I found that these external rewards were not enough to keep me participating in office politics any longer, or to force me to fit someone else's idea of who I was and allow them to put me in a box where I looked like everyone else. My inquisitive nature got the best of me, as I was hungry for more and for a different perspective. The more I become aware of this, the more I made people uncomfortable, including myself at times as well.

For with understanding your true self, your strengths, and your ability to lead also comes a great responsibility to walk the talk and lead by example. It takes courage, commitment, and perseverance to step up and challenge the status quo.

Don't get me wrong, I liked to push the boundaries, and often took on the role of playing devil's advocate with what was simply accepted and comfortable. I would challenge other leaders when something was unclear or seemed misaligned with our overall vision. I would lead my own teams boldly and with the freedom to be different and to give themselves permission to fail. I was told I was too transparent with them. Perhaps that was so. I had creative, innovative, and new approaches to how I chose to lead my teams. I wanted to empower them to stretch out of their comfort zones, to be more.

As a result, the teams I led were successful, and I found myself rocking the boat a lot!

I remember one meeting in particular with a higher-ranking manager, when we were working on a project and it was apparent how different our styles were. As we were discussing ways in which we could leverage each other's strengths and work differently with each other, she said to me, "Candy, you are too big of a thinker, you are too passionate, and too transparent with your teams. I think you might want to adapt your approach and not play so big."

Not play so big? I remember sitting there trying not to smile at her comment. I knew she was coming from a well-intentioned place as she spoke those words. She believed what she was saying to me, trying to be a coach and mentor to me, and she thought she was giving me the tools and perspective to "win." In her mind, she was taking responsibility to have a crucial conversation with me. However, as much as I tried to conceal my reaction (I tend to wear my emotions on my sleeve—another one of my "toos"), she noticed my facial expression and questioned me about it.

I simply responded that while I appreciated where her comment was coming from (I truly did, as I knew she was not trying to be malicious by any means, she only was trying to coach me on something she thought would help further me in my career with the company from *her* perspective), and I knew that she really wanted the best for me, all I heard her say in that comment she offered was "strength, strength, strength." You see, for me, these were the *very* qualities that made me stand out and were attractive to the company when it recruited me years back. Now, as I once again started to make others nervous, they were the same qualities that, out of fear, they wanted to squash or tone down.

You see, I finally realized for myself that all those "toos" that kept being called to my attention were exactly the core essence of who I am and are not up for compromise. I take great pride in having passion about the work I do, the teams I lead, and the impact I create.

I believe in being direct and honest with people whenever and however possible, and being transparent above all else. And unless something is confidential or a legal issue, then I believe in having open communication with my team. I take great pride in the fact that I was labeled "transparent to a fault" (as many a performance review indicated). For my transparency illustrates my authenticity and my genuine trust in others, especially my teams, as well as their trust in me.

As for thinking big, that one just baffles me. And as I still try to wrap my head around why this is such a threat, I am quickly reminded of how many people try to *lead* from a place of fear versus trust. The rub, or irony, is that one cannot lead from fear—one can only manage when one allows fear to be a driving factor. Process and things are to be managed, people are not.

Leadership comes from a place of trust and abundance. Fear negates the very idea of leadership and allows one to only manage, and usually micromanage people instead. Leaders are open to being challenged and to being vulnerable. They give trust freely and allow room for their teams to empower themselves to be challenged, to become leaders themselves, and to grow in their individual strengths and capabilities. Leadership is about growth and stretching the comfort zone of an organization—to try new things, test the waters, lead by example, and create positive momentum for others.

For vulnerability is not a sign of weakness, but rather a great source of strength. Many claim to want to build teams of people who are smarter, more daring, and bigger thinkers, yet, when push comes to shove, these qualities scare them to the very core, and they end up doing the exact opposite. They end up micromanaging, stifling creativity, and limiting their teams to do only what always has been done before. You hear expressions all the time like, "Well, this is the way we always have approached this," or "We don't have resources to try something new." Wow, how limiting that becomes both when trying to be innovative and competitive in the marketplace and in growing new leaders.

As a leader, I was oftentimes quite unorthodox in my approach and in the freedom I gave my team to grow. I was blessed at several points in my career to be mentored by other leaders who were more daring and abundant themselves, freely giving me the space and trust to truly lead my teams. I was able to recruit and build teams based on members' individual strengths, and highlight how together, as a team, they created something more amazing and more impactful than as individual contributors. Something much bigger, better, and smarter than me, for sure.

I would argue that every person on my teams was smarter, more creative, and more talented than me. I learned as much, if not more, from these people as they did from me. I believe my role was to lead others and grow people that are empowered to understand and maximize their own talents and establish a strong sense of self. When given that opportunity, people desire to maximize their own performance and to crave achieving greater impact. All you have to do is get out of their way and provide the means to help them shine.

As I began to assess all the ways the "too" box started to grow around me, I went through my own journey and self-assessment of what truly makes my heart dance, and I realized, for me, my next step was outside the walls of the corporate structure. My "toos" were my gifts to share with others to help them find their own way. So, here I am today as life strategies and accountability coach, business consultant, author, and motivational speaker, where my "toos" have become the very tools I leverage and share with clients, with friends, and with my community.

Now, it took me a while to realize what my purpose is and to build a life affording me every opportunity to do just that. Like many, I was limited, for a long time, in my own beliefs, along with my need to excel and prove something to myself and to others. I thought it was up to me to win the game, rather than create a whole new playbook and space for myself instead. Once I realized that I would rather celebrate my strengths and fight to live my dream, I stopped worrying so much about working toward someone else's.

With that focus and decision, I moved myself cross-country from Milwaukee to Austin and started my own business coaching others to do more, be more, and achieve more. Never have I looked back with regret, for I gladly take responsibility for the choices I have made. My future is bright and I have the power within me to make it whatever I want it to be.

Not unlike my own trials and tribulations over the years, you also have the ability to break free from the constraints of what you think you should be, and truly set yourself free for the magnificent light you were destined to shine. It may be a different role at work, or maybe doing your current role in a different, more impactful, personally rewarding way, or venturing out on your own as I did. There are infinite options when you give yourself the permission to play big.

Whatever it is, the answer lies within you. We all have within us a song that is ours to sing, and only ours to sing. Our only purpose on this earth is to give that song a melody, a harmony, and an orchestra all its own, so that it can be heard and appreciated by others.

If you are ready, let's begin to take the steps that will release the song that lives within the depths of your soul and free the music that sits within your heart. Whether it be finding the way to be your authentic self at home, at work, or to find your life's purpose that sits outside the preverbal box, as in any process, there always are steps to take to ensure you will be successful in your quest. This book is designed to give you those steps in a simple and comprehensive way. The first step we will be working through together is to define your *why*. But before we can even do that, I must first help you find your *way* ...

"When I let go of what I am, I become what I might be."
– Lao Tzu

Call to Action

1) Approach this book with an open mind and open heart. Dare to dream and think outside your current frame. Give yourself permission to feel the experience as you go through it, and to stretch your current limitations.

2) Take time to do the exercises at the end of each chapter. They are designed to help you challenge yourself, ask yourself the tough questions that need to be asked, and provide you with greater insight into what you really want. In taking time to do the work, you will be able to build the best road map for you to navigate yourself to your ultimate destination.

two

Finding 'The' Way

"Determination is the wake-up call to the human will"
- Anthony Robbins

"Where there is a will, there is a Candy Barone!" For those of you who don't know me, let me introduce myself—my name is Candy Barone. Yes, the same person who is the author for this book. This statement, my mantra really, is one that I tell myself at every crossroads, at every challenge, at every turning point, just about every day. For truly it is that simple. "Where there is a will ...," my friend, there is a YOU!

YOU are the only "way" there is to make things happen in your life. Sure, you may need other resources, or enlist others for help at times, but the ultimate choice to do something, anything, is up to you, and you alone. YOU have the power to decide. You decide which road to take, which option is best, whether you will take action or not, how you respond to people, situations, and circumstances. The choice is YOURS to make. Yet, so many times we give away that power, we blame others for our own current situation, and we feel helpless in our own lives and in the perceived *lack* of choices.

I am here to tell you that *now* is the time to change that thinking. *Now* is the time to maximize your ability to choose. *Now* is the time to learn how to empower yourself for more, and to decide that *you* deserve better than settling for less.

You are designed to accomplish great things. Yet, somehow we falter in the eyes of adversity, we lose our faith in our ability to overcome and persevere, and we forget how powerful and talented we truly are. We allow ourselves to fall victim to circumstance and our environment, versus embracing challenges as gifts and opportunities. We are given trials and tribulations to showcase our strengths, not diminish them.

God has given you all the tools you need to succeed, to triumph in what may be perceived as darkness, and to win in the battles that come your way. The challenges you face are meant to strengthen you, to lift you up, and to clearly show you your own internal power to succeed. They are experiences designed to help you grow, evolve, and fine-tune your own sense of self. As hard as challenges may become, as dark as it may seem, your light from within is there for you to shine. That light, YOUR light, can make miracles happen. It's only a matter of learning how to adjust your filters and how to remove your barriers that will give you full access to the magnificent light within you to fully allow it to shine in all its radiance and brilliance.

At times, we all get stuck, and I get that (and, honestly, I have my moments, too, for it is human nature to doubt, have fear, and have "off" days). We all lose sight of what matters most, as we allow life, what we've been told, others' judgments, what we've learned from others and ourselves, prior experiences, our environment, and our own beliefs to indicate how we see ourselves, how we value our own worth.

By doing this, we shift our power to something we cannot control, or worse, something that limits our own belief in what's possible. We allow outside influences to write our own script rather than create our own masterpiece. YOU are the conductor to your orchestra, the one specifically and magnificently designed for you. It is up to you to build that orchestra and unleash the music within, to create the score that will allow you to play the song that is uniquely yours to reveal. It's just a matter of assembling your orchestra and teaching it the right song to play.

I wrote a poem many years ago that I still use as my personal vision statement today. In fact, when I took Stephen Covey's training based on his book "The 7 Habits of Highly Effective People", and we had to write out our vision statement, I realized that I had already written mine. So, I am sharing it with you today in hopes that it will provide a new way to envision your own life, and the choices that are yours to make.

Take a moment to visualize the words from the poem I wrote, the sounds you hear, the colors described, and how you would visualize your own orchestra or band coming to life. What music would you play? What instruments would you assemble? What would it sound like, feel like?

I ask you, conductor, are you ready to play your song?

Orchestra of Life

The music begins to play.
Lessons of yesterday,
Realities of today,
Promises of tomorrow
Set forth the composition for destiny.
The orchestra directs a collage of colors to assemble.
Strength and courage resonate from the brass ensemble.
Sorrows and pain emanate from the string quartet.
Life's purest melody expelled from keys of ivory and black.
In the echoes of darkness, light can be found.
Sweet harmony is released.
Arrays of color fuse together.
In one breath, hues are not separate
Light and darkness are the same.
A single shade of hope is evident.
Vivid and decadent the strand of life transforms.
Neither from sight, nor sound
Does the brilliance become conceivable?

The senses become diluted.
Peace within marks the distinction of the moment.
To savor, to comprehend,
Is in the sole power of the conductor.
Conductor, play your song.

As you can see, your vision can take shape any way that makes the most sense to you. So, now it's your turn. Take time to create your own vision, in whatever form you want it to take (could be a poem, a song, a statement, or something entirely different—the point is to make it *yours*). But the challenge is to give it life. The more you envision it, feel it, and can describe it, the more your own subconscious begins to own it.

You see, you have a very powerful imagination. And when you put that imagination to work in a way that creates your dreams, breathes life into your hopes and desires, you begin to become more intentional about the actions in your life you are taking. You start to align your goals and dreams to the very things you do each and every day. Your imagination is a powerful tool to help you create congruence in your life between what you say you really want and how you go about bringing that to reality.

For this is truly *your* way. Where there's a will, there is *you*, your imagination, your ability to shape your subconscious differently and purposefully, and to become the conductor of your personal orchestra. There is no limit to what you can create for yourself if you are willing and learn how to master the tools within yourself.

Now that we have talked about finding the way (keep telling yourself, "Where there is a will ..." there is what? A *you*! And, I challenge you to take that one step further, and say, "Where there's a will, there is a [insert your name]), it's now time to define your why.

Your *why* is one of the most critical elements to creating a successful road map and creating personal accountability. For, if you don't acknowledge what's in it for you, and what is your compelling reason to create change in your life, then how will you stay motivated to put in the work required? What is the emotional connection that makes this change so relevant and important to you? Why do you choose to be different? Why now? What will happen in your life as a result, if you do? What if you don't?

Understanding your *why* is critical to creating a sustainable plan that allows you to be successful. For, when things get tough and the challenge of change itself becomes difficult (and they likely will at some point, or several times, in your journey), you need to remind yourself and bring yourself back to what your compelling *why* is, in order to stay the course. If your *why* doesn't have an emotional connection tied to it, the probability of its being your true reason is extremely low. Your compelling *why* should provoke an emotional response, both in whether you accomplish the desired goal and if you don't. How does it impact other areas of your life, or who you are?

After we define your *why* in the next chapter, we will then spend some time together in the chapters that follow laying out a road map, and then understanding the things that could be slowing you down, standing in your way, or simply sabotaging you completely and stopping you from getting what you truly want.

"Life is 10% what happens to me and 90% of how I react to it."
– John Maxwell

Call to Action

1) Think about those times in your life when you didn't go after your dreams, when you limited yourself from doing more, or you let yourself be put in a "box" based on someone else's expectations or fear. What did it cost you? How did you feel about yourself? Did you feel empowered, or as if you gave power away?

2) Now, ask yourself: "If you could have a do-over, how would you be different? What would you have done instead, or liked to have done? Take some time to think about this and envision a different script than the one you actually lived. Give yourself permission to create a new visual of the outcome and your choices.

3) Start by telling yourself, "Where there's a will, there is a (insert *your* name). Or better yet, create your own mantra that encompasses the words that give you fire, keep you motivated and focused in times of adversity. Write your mantra (or borrow mine) and repeat to yourself several times throughout the day and ALWAYS during times of trials and tribulations. Use this mantra every day, and any time you find yourself stuck, frustrated, or unsure.

4) Look back on your life to a time when you accomplished something great (we all have—so, don't cop out here) or when you overcame a huge obstacle … What are the words and actions you used to persevere during that time, or when things got tough? How do you channel your inner voice to make things happen?

5) Now that you have solidified your mantra, create a vision "statement" for yourself. This can be in whatever form you desire—a poem, a song, a statement, a picture … the possibilities are endless. Make it come to life any way that makes sense to you. Give yourself permission to play, pretend you are a child playing a game of "what if."

6) Use your creativity to unlock and uncover the way you can best visualize how you see your life and how you see your role to be

the conductor in your own orchestra. Make it YOURS! Take time to describe it through words or colors, any way in which you can truly bring it to life and visualize it for yourself. Think about how you would describe it to someone else?

7) Share your vision with someone else, a trusted friend, advisor, mentor, or family member. Create greater personal accountability around who you want to be and how you envision your life. Hang your vision "statement" in a place where you can see it regularly. Take some time to read it to yourself every day, hear the words, see the picture. Make it real.

three

Where There's a Will and a Way, There Better Be a Why

"An unexamined life is not worth living."
–Socrates

It is imperative that before you start any journey involving change, you first need to understand the reason and desire behind wanting this change. If you don't know and fully understand what's in it for you, why it matters, and why it is important to you, then you are sunk before you even start to set sail.

Ownership in your journey starts with knowing where you currently are, at this particular moment in your life, where you want to be going, having a vision as to what you desire most and want in your life, and why that matters. What compels you to want to change? What motivates and inspires you for more? What's in it for you? What is the cost if you don't do something differently? What is the reward when you accomplish your goal? What ultimately is your "why?"

As I mentioned in the last chapter, it is important that your compelling *why* be connected to an emotional response. The only way to ensure you stay in the game, and keep your goal in front of you, is to understand the emotion that is driving you to want the change in the first place. Without it, your *why* is empty and I would bet that you still haven't taken the risk to be vulnerable in your real compelling *why*.

What is the magnificent desire that your heart holds? If money were no object, if priorities didn't exist, if barriers weren't there, if all the "*what if*" factors weren't present, what would you do? Who would you decide to be? How would you spend your time? Who would be impacted? Who would be with you as you travel on your journey? Why does that matter? How would that impact your life?

As I have coached many people to better understand their *why*, I created a series of questions to help navigate them through this discovery process. These questions were designed to better understand what really is in your heart. What do you want most? What do you want to stop doing?

I also recommend that you allow yourself the freedom to be courageous and remove your normal filters when answering these questions. This exercise is to help you tap into your deepest desires, your unyielding and most magnificent passion. Forget about what you think the "right" answer should be, or what you think others might think or say, or how what you want doesn't fit in your existing life and priorities. This is your opportunity to dream as big as you want. We need to build the dream first before we can create a road map to get you there.

Remember the discussion around letting your imagination work its magic. Be childlike in your quest; remove all your adult, learned behaviors and thinking. Let your imagination soar, much like the eagle, above the storm of your everyday life. Don't put edges or boundaries on what your imagination wants to naturally do. Be free and let it fly without direction. Capture the essence of every shape, color, feeling, thought. Unburden your mind and heart from all your responsibilities and give yourself the freedom to put your imagination in the driver's seat for this exercise.

This is a time to remove all that noise, all those barriers, and just be. No filters or presumptions are allowed in this exercise. No bias of who you are or how you perceive yourself to be today. Trust me (and yourself), as there is no right or wrong answer—just dream it. Take yourself back to being a kid and play make-believe for a moment.

Now, take some real time to "build your dream" and think as big as your imagination and heart will let you. Truly, a blue-sky, fun exercise to "play" and just be. No rules, no boundaries, no expectations—this is for you and you alone. Pretend you are a superhero or have superpowers (which you do, in all reality ... but we will talk more about that later). This is the land of "make-believe" and "where dreams really do come true."

Also, note that these questions may require that you to work through them multiple times. At first, as much as you want to be free and allow yourself space to dream, you might just be scratching the surface. You have years of learned adult thinking and "rules" you have established for yourself to set free. Only with deeper inspection, greater reflection, and tremendous honesty will you start to pull the layers back and get to the heart of what fuels you.

I challenge you to go through this exercise a few times, giving yourself some space in between each iteration. Don't get frustrated if the answers don't come right away, or if you have to spend more time than you thought in finding your truths. You have not failed; this is all part of the exploration process! Take all the time you need. Understanding where you get your energy, what drains you, what matters to you, all are so important in creating the right road map to take you where you want to go. It also helps to identify potential barriers that could be getting in your way right now.

Keep in mind that this is not an exercise you give your brain and heart often; you are purposefully thinking differently, more broadly, and expansively. Embrace the journey, all of it, for there is great introspection in the answers you will uncover. And part of the magic is in the process itself.

With that being said, let the child in you lead the adult. Be creative, explore, dream. Here are the questions I want you to start thinking about and challenge yourself with:

- What excites you? What are you most passionate about?
- What strengths do you feel you bring to your job, to your work, to your team, to your relationships, to your community?
- What do you know about yourself that you feel you don't do well? How do you deal with that? What are you challenged by?
- What drains you in a given day? How do you react to overwhelming challenges, burdens, responsibilities, and stress?
- What's the one accomplishment you are most proud of? Think through some of your professional and personal milestones. What is the one thing you would have done differently, if given a do-over?
- Think back over your career and identify a moment when you believe you were performing at your personal best. Why does this moment stand out? What competencies were you using at the time? How did this make you feel?

There also are two quotes I want you to consider. The first is from a program called "Spiritual Madness"; the second from "Conversations with God." I share these quotes and the questions that follow with you because I found them useful in coaching others and in helping me, personally, identify the person I wanted to be as I went through my own journey, and continue to explore my true self every day.

"The heart of madness is wanting life to be other than it is, to be humanly logical; wanting the chaos to end. But chaos is change and change offers the possibility for growth and growth is almost always good."

"You are the creator of your reality, and life can show up no other way for you than that way in which you think it will."

So, the questions really focus on: who are you really, as a human being? As you reflect on those two statements, ask yourself:

- What is it that I can do any time of day or night, no matter how tired I am, no matter what else is going on in my life? Something that "feeds" me; something I simply must do?

- What "experience" creates or elicits the feeling of being completely at home for me—that thing that is most completely, essentially me?

Take time to understand what really is in your heart. Again, take all the time you need. This is not an exercise to rush through, as it lays the framework for all the work you will be putting in to make these dreams a reality. If you don't have a true sense of your destination, then it matters little what path or course you choose to take.

The more you can fine-tune *what* you want, what gives you energy (as well as what drains you), the more you can create the best road map to navigate your path to reach that destination. This is the hardest part of your journey, for once you set your compass due north, you will be much more likely to stay the course.

• • •

Now that you have gone through this exercise, hopefully a couple of times now, how are you feeling? What was the most surprising aha for you? Did anything catch you off guard or simply throw you off balance? Do you feel you are living your life in congruence with the answers you uncovered and where you get your energy from?

Where did you find yourself most unbalanced or misaligned? Were you able to uncover any patterns around where you get energy and where your energy is drained? What does that say about your life today? Are you doing the things you enjoy most? What does it tell you about what you really want?

I use this exercise with every client I coach. One client in particular whom I was coaching continued to stress his desire to do more, be more, and make more. We were working on revising his résumé and looking at new career opportunities for him. He was frustrated and couldn't understand why he felt stuck in his current job and career overall. I gave him these questions and had him work on them in his own time. I asked him to bring them back to our follow-up session a week later. He did just that.

As we proceeded to dig into his responses, a pattern started to emerge. It became very clear that this client had a passion for helping others, developing people, and helping organizations manage change. However, as we were discussing where he got his energy from, and what his true passions really were, he also stated (in almost the same breath) that he had put his résumé out for several sales positions hoping for a bite. Hmmm, I sensed an area where he was misaligned and incongruent with what we uncovered as his true desires and what he actually was spending the majority of his time and focus on.

I asked him to pause for a moment and repeat what he had just said to me. So, he did, more slowly this time. When he said the same thing again, I responded, "I'm curious, how will a new sales position give you the opportunity to develop people and help organizations through change? I only ask because, as I have been in both roles myself, I am not sure I see the connection." It was as if a lightbulb went off instantly. My client paused, and said, "Wow, I never thought about it like that ... I don't think it does. Wait, then maybe I need to be approaching this differently."

We continued to talk this new idea over, and he came to the conclusion that he still needed to revise his résumé, but now, not to highlight his ability to sell, but rather highlight his ability to coach and develop people, along with making decisions to help organizations navigate through change.

You see, he had these skills and expertise in his wheelhouse already, but he never was focused on them because he always went after sales positions, because that was all he was used to doing. It never occurred to him to highlight the areas he really was interested in and approach his career differently. It never occurred to him because he was trapped in the framework and thinking he always had used.

Sometimes it is just that easy sometimes all we need is a mirror to be held up for us to see how we are getting in our own way. Sometimes it takes much more work to uncover what truly is getting in your way and where you are being the most incongruent in your life. Either way, the process for discovery remains the same.

Since then, my client has restructured his road map (and résumé) and is working on moving toward the things that give him the most energy and passion. He no longer is seeking to find a sales position, but for leadership roles where he can expand his skills in developing others and helping organizations manage through change for growth.

By understanding the areas where you are out of balance and not being congruent in your life, you will start to create a better, more aligned plan to address those gaps. Awareness of what is getting in your way is the first step in creating your personal blueprint to live the life you were meant to live. The answers you uncover are your true self telling you what it wants most. Now, it is up to you to decide if you are ready to embrace change to make those dreams become a reality.

Anything is possible if you want it badly enough and you fully understand your "why?" Even if you are asking yourself, "How can that be, I have so many responsibilities and priorities that I can't even spare the time to 'dream' about what I really want?" If it is truly important to you, you will make time.

I am here to tell you, it IS possible. You can meet your commitments and responsibilities and STILL live your dream to the fullest. All it takes is belief, a plan, and a system to hold yourself accountable. Are you ready?

"In order to succeed, your desire for success should be greater than your fear of failure."
– Bill Cosby

Call to Action

1) Take time to answer these questions honestly and deeply without filters or expectations. Release all your current limitations as you explore what is possible. Let the child in you out to play, imagine, create, and dream. Give yourself the space and time for reflection and multiple iterations as you answer these questions for yourself.

   - What excites you? What are you most passionate about?
   - What strengths do you feel you bring to your job, to your work, to your team, your relationships, your family, your community?
   - What do you know about yourself that you feel you don't do well? How do you deal with that? What are you challenged by?
   - What drains you in a given day? How do you react to overwhelming challenges, burdens, responsibilities, and stress?
   - What's the one accomplishment you are most proud of? Discuss some of your professional milestones. What is the one thing you would have done differently, if given a do-over?
   - Think back over your career and identify a moment when you believe you were performing at your personal best. Why does this moment stand out? What competencies were you using at the time? How did this make you feel?

2) Reflect on these two quotes and answer the following questions:

   - "The heart of madness is wanting life to be other than it is, to be humanly logical; wanting the chaos to end. But chaos is change and change offers the possibility for growth and growth is almost always good."
   - "You are the creator of your reality, and life can show up no other way for you than that way in which you think it will."
   - So, the questions are centered on "who am I really, as a human being?" Ask yourself these questions:

- What is it that I can do any time of day or night, no matter how tired I am, no matter what else is going on in my life? Something that "feeds" me; something I simply must do?

- What "experience" creates or elicits the feeling of being completely at home for me—that thing that is most completely, essentially me?

3) Assess how you are feeling after going through the questions. Did anything in particular stand out? Were there any big ahas you uncovered?

4) Identify patterns that emerged around what gives you energy and what drains you? Are you being congruent in your life today with what you enjoy most? What seems to be your biggest gap or the barrier standing in your way most? How might you begin to address those gaps?

four

Get Off the Treadmill and Build a New Road

"Start where you are. Use what you have. Do what you can."
– Arthur Ashe

Do you ever find yourself going, going, going … only to find out that you either are running in circles or the road you are running on actually is a treadmill? And the more you try to run, the harder and faster you try to run, the more you find yourself stuck in the same spot?

What if you could create a new and exciting road to run on instead? What if you didn't have to run at all, but could find more enjoyable and creative ways to arrive at your destination? What if you could bring others along in your journey to help support you and experience the ride with you?

What do you want to achieve? Do you have a clear vision about what you truly want and the meaning behind why you have that vision? If not, I recommend you spend some more time working through the exercises in Chapters 1–3 to help you gain greater clarity and understanding of what you truly want and your compelling *why*. In order for the next few chapters to really be helpful and impactful, it is important to be clear about where you are trying to go.

Once you do have a clear vision, we need to then start to break down what has been holding you back from that dream and the vision you created about the life you most desire. But first, before we do that, let's start with your commitment to self. Are you ready? Are you ready to take the steps necessary to achieve the goals you want? Commitment to self is the first, and most crucial, step in your ability and desire to hold yourself personally accountable in every step of the process.

In the book *No Excuses: The Power of Self-Discipline*, Brian Tracy talks about how to take on the greatest form of self-discipline and personal accountability by using three words in every situation. He claims by telling yourself, "I am responsible" no matter what the circumstances are, even if it's just in the way you choose to react, you are able to change everything about your current perspective and take full accountability for being able to make choices in your life and for owning the outcomes when you do.

I challenge you to say that phrase to yourself every time you feel the opportunity to play the victim, or feel like you have lost all control of the choices in your life, and of your life itself. "I am responsible" demonstrates your unwillingness to let other things dictate whether things will or will not be in your life.

You also become unwilling to allow those circumstances to define your *way. You* are your way; therefore, *you* are responsible to make it happen and to create the life you want. Make a choice as to whether you want to be amazing or simply average! Dare to be great! Why be someone who lives by everyone else's insecurities, barriers, limitations, and fears? Why not be the person to blaze a new path and show others what is truly possible?

It is your destiny to be great and shine the light that is uniquely yours! But it also is up to *you* to decide whether you want that choice. For it is a gift, and yours to have, but with it also comes responsibility and personal accountability. If you do decide to go all in and accept the terms, then you are in for a magical and wonderful ride!

Now, I guarantee, regardless of making the commitment to accept your destiny, you will falter and make mistakes along the way. We all make mistakes. It is human to err. What you do with those setbacks and how you react to them will ultimately dictate how successful you are in this quest. Again, keep telling yourself, "I am responsible."

Failing is part of the process. Accept that and release that. The more you anchor yourself by that fear, the more you remain stuck. Failing is nothing more than stretching your own current limitations. You will never know what you are capable of unless you stumble, fall, and learn how to pick yourself up. You need to remind yourself how to bounce back when you fail. You need to challenge yourself to push outside of your comfort zone, and you only can do that by failing first.

Our failures give us a reflection of what is holding us back, what is getting in our way, and what limiting ways of thinking we still hold onto that need to change. Failing is a gift that allows you to try something different. As we know, the definition of insanity is doing the same thing over and over again expecting to get a different result. In failing, we are forced to try a different approach, to reset our thinking, to learn from what didn't work.

Failing, however, is *not* a reflection of who you are as a person. It is a function of stretching yourself outside of what you currently know. It is about the work, the step, the attempt … it is not about your worth. Failing is not meant to serve as a tactic that we should internalize and beat ourselves up about over and over and over again.

Learn from what makes you stumble, embrace the opportunity for reflection, and honor the ability to try something else on, to see a different way to get there. Wasting countless hours berating yourself will not create a more abundant future. Internalizing the failure as a reflection of self will only perpetuate more negativity and fear.

Release the urge to beat yourself down, to validate the fears that have held you back in the first place. Be grateful for the experience and the learning opportunity. Understand how and where you can pay those lessons forward to others, and for yourself. Keep the vision in sight and remember the compelling "why" you defined when the roadblocks and hurdles present themselves. And, trust me, they will. But know you are stronger than the trials and tribulations. You are only given what you truly can handle, even if you can't see the end in sight.

Remember, it's not about climbing the entire staircase at once, but about taking the first step, then the next, and the next one after that. Before long, you will look down and realize you climbed halfway to the top! Celebrate the climb during the climb, too. Make sure to set up rewards along the way (you will learn some tools to manage your fear of failure and set up ways to celebrate in Chapter 10).

Know that the process will require work, but that change can begin to happen immediately. Change your perspective and change will happen. Though there are no shortcuts in creating the life you want, and you will need to do the work to bring the things you desire most forward in your life, all of this is possible and attainable. You will need to be present and aware of the choices you make. Again, you are responsible.

There are ways to call more abundance to you, to make your dreams a reality more and more every day. Keep working, stay the course, and do whatever it takes to believe it *can* happen. The old saying "fake it until you make it" applies here. The more you believe in what is possible, live your life as if you already have achieved your goals, and change your actions to be more intentional in achieving those dreams, the more you will see and experience positive outcomes and the results you want.

Change your frame from "I wish" and "I want" to "I am" and "I have" and you start to also change your actions. You become more intentional when you believe something already *is* versus when you only hope it might happen.

There will be times when you feel like you are indecisive and don't know how to decide the right next step. Those are the opportunities when you simply need to make a decision. Being indecisive creates delay and frustration. If you allow it to fester too long, it creates a vicious circle that breeds worry and opportunities for you to lament over days lost. Decide to do something, *anything*. By deciding to do something, you simultaneously decide not to do something else. Sometimes half the battle is won in simply making a decision.

You always can change direction or make a different decision later, if you find the one you made no longer serves. But don't allow yourself to become paralyzed in making a decision in the first place. A decision today does *not* have to be the same decision for tomorrow. Making a choice, solidifying a decision, provides you with a sense of empowerment, knowledge that you are capable. You make decisions every day; trust your ability to do so. Sometimes just making a decision, any decision, helps us from being stuck and frees us to open up our thinking once again.

"OK, I get all that," you might be saying to yourself, "but how and where do I really start?" Great question, and let's break this down. Once you have established *what* it is you are trying to change, and then have fully understood your *why* around that end state, the next step is to break the desired outcome into bite-size pieces.

Again, it is not about tackling the staircase in one-fell swoop. Instead, it is about creating small and achievable milestones where you can gauge your progress, stop and take inventory to make sure you still are aligned with your overall goals, and create rewards for yourself and the achievements made (even small ones get rewarded). This model creates a sustainable process that will help keep you on course.

Create a time frame as to when you want a desired outcome or change to occur. Make sure to be realistic, but aggressive enough to push yourself toward action, as this creates desire and doesn't give you the opportunity to either feel defeated before you even get started or bored in the middle of the journey. Once the time frame is determined, then think about all the steps required to get there (some of you may not know at this point—that's all right, give yourself a placeholder for the "unknowns").

Start to back out all the steps across your time frame, starting with today. Identify your first step. Then pause and ask yourself, "Is this really my first step or do I need to do something else first?"

I have you go through that exercise because oftentimes our current thinking or limited beliefs tell us we "should" start here, when in reality, we are not prepared for that step yet. Let me give you an example:

You have decided that you want to make a career change. You have been in sales for a long time and find that you are unhappy, even though you seem to do fairly well in that role. You have updated your résumé and are looking for new jobs.

However, when you go through the questions in Chapter 3: "Where There's a Will and a Way, There Better Be a Why," you realize that your passion is around helping to grow people and you get energy in helping organizing work through change (just like the client I told you about). What you currently are doing and seeking seems incongruent with what your heart really wants.

So, you decide the first step then is to update your résumé to show all the skills you possess and experience you have had in developing both people and organizations. You know this is your first step. However, when you sit at your computer, you find yourself frozen. You start to feel even more stuck. You begin to ask yourself questions like, "What skills do I possess that would indicate my experience in this area? What are companies looking for? How would I go about restructuring my entire résumé to reflect this?" You panic; it all seems so daunting and complicated.

You decide, "Whatever, I have a resume and I will just look for another sales position … maybe it's just the company I work for, or I am bored with the product I sell, or …"

Do you see what happened there? Because your first step was too big and too daunting, you decided to throw in the towel and continue doing what you've always been doing. You start to second-guess your objective, your desire, your passion. You make excuses or cover up the core reason you are so unhappy. You give away control to your environment and circumstances.

So, what could you do differently, you might ask. Take a step back to reevaluate why you are stuck. Why does this task seem so daunting? Is it the right step to start with? Maybe, instead, you need to do some research. Maybe you need to search the Internet, ask recruiters or friends in those types of roles or ask hiring managers as to what they are looking for in qualified candidates. What skills and experiences are desired to best illustrate your capacity to lead? Are there things outside of work that give you those skills (e.g., think community work, board positions, outside projects, or hobbies, etc.).

What about revising the résumé itself? Is this a skill or requirement that uses your talent to its best and highest ability? Are you able to outsource the changes to someone who does this regularly and enjoys the work? Are there people within your network that you can connect with to get introductions or assistance in your search?

Do you see how your first step might need to be broken down further into something more tangible and manageable? We often-times set ourselves up with expectations and demands that are so taxing that we lose sight of what we were trying to accomplish in the first place.

Break down your first step into smaller bites. Here's another way to look at this: when someone is trying to lose a lot of weight (say fifty to one hundred pounds.), there is a reason why so much focus is placed on losing the first ten pounds. That is the first major (or minor, depending on how you frame it) hurdle to cross. It is a small-enough goal that it is doable in a reasonable amount of time, and yet aggressive enough to make a difference. Once someone loses his or her first ten pounds, the chances for continued success go up drastically.

The momentum has been started and the person is in the process of learning, accepting, and adopting the new behavior.

It's all about getting the momentum going in the right direction and taking the very first step on the staircase of life. Lay out all the major milestones and break each one down further, where you can, with the steps needed to accomplish it. Remember, one foot, or goal, in front of another. Then repeat and follow the same strategy again.

Allow for flexibility in the plan, too. Sometimes we spend so much time watching the front door for opportunity to knock and enter that we lose sight of opportunity when it presents itself in other ways. Maybe it comes in the back door, a window, or doesn't come into the house at all. Maybe it is in your garden, or around a corner, or in the most unusual and unexpected place. The point is to remain open and flexible throughout the process. Don't get locked in or fixate to the point where you are unable to make adjustments, corrections, or modifications where needed.

So, create your road map, but don't be locked *in* your road map. Use it as a navigational tool that allows for alternate routes (even your GPS device gives you options to take, in case of construction or traffic, or maybe you just want a more scenic route).

You may find new and exciting ways to make your reality happen—that is the best part about the journey! Once you start to put your road map or navigational guide together, we need to check your self-talk next to make sure you are not putting yourself at risk in sabotaging yourself with the thoughts and words you use along the way. Now, let's talk about becoming more intentional …

"Two roads diverged in a wood, and I took the one
less traveled by, and that has made all the difference."
–Robert Frost

Call to Action

1) Make a commitment to yourself to be great and live the destiny you deserve. Connect this commitment back to your *why* and create and visualize what accomplishing this looks like in your mind's eye.

2) Accept responsibility for your choices and reactions to the circumstances in your life. Choose not to play a victim or martyr in your life. Repeat these words to yourself often, "I am responsible."

3) Understand failing and mistakes are part of the process; and embrace them. Acknowledge that they are part of the journey, and that failing is simply permission to try something else.

4) Change the frame you currently are using to one that creates purpose and action, which assumes you already have achieved your desired outcome. Reframe the words you use from "I will" and "I want" to "I am" and "I have."

5) Identify the time frame you want to achieve your final goal. Make it realistic, but somewhat aggressive to give you something to stretch for. Create action immediately and celebrate small wins right away.

6) Break your goal down into bite-size pieces and back out across your timeline into realistic milestones. Create placeholders for any steps that still are unknown to allow yourself the space and freedom to add or change direction along the way.

7) Identify your first step. Then pause and ask yourself, "Is this really my first step, or is there something else I need to do before I can make that happen?" You might have to break your *first* step down even further to get momentum moving forward.

8) Make a decision and take action! It is important to get the momentum going. Allow yourself freedom to know that a decision can

be changed later to help from getting stuck. A decision is better than no decision—it creates action, and action is the only way you will get closer to your goal.

five

The Power and Intention of the Words You Choose

"We become what we think about."
– Earl Nightingale

Do you believe there is power in the words you choose? Are you intentional about the words you choose when communicating with others? What about with yourself?

You probably have heard the adage: "you become what you think." Did you know that while that holds very true, you actually not only become what you think, you also become what you say to yourself, and believe about yourself, as well?

In addition, you also become everything you choose to internalize from your environment, outside influences, and what others think (or what you *think* they think about you) and speak. What you hold to be true (whether positive or negative) is what you start to believe, both consciously and unconsciously.

Whether you are influenced by the words of those you surround yourself with, the judgments passed that you acknowledge and unwittingly validate about yourself, or the internal dialogue in your own mind, you give power to what you think most about, what you speak about, what you dream about.

Wow, can you see where this can start to become a merciless cycle that you continue to perpetuate if you are not intentional about what you are feeding your mind and soul?

The universe gives you *whatever* you ask for, whether you believe this or not. You matriculate and call to you that which you give the most energy to. Ask yourself, "Am I being intentional about my own self talk? "Am I treating myself the way I want others to treat me? What energy am I creating for myself?" Take a moment to reflect on your own patterns and decide whether you are more intentional about the words you use with strangers, friends, and loved ones versus the ones you choose to use for yourself?

So, how does *your* internal dialogue go?

Let me give you an example of what typically happens: You have a friend that calls you, stressed, frustrated, and seemingly very negative. Your friend says something along the lines of: "UGH, today sucks!!! I totally screwed up big time. I am so stupid! I have no idea why they hired me, I can't do anything right!**"**

Now, likely, you are not going to continue the cycle of self-deprecation your friends have started to build around themselves and berate them further. No, instead you are going to do everything you can to try and lift them back up, to encourage them, to help get them out of their own way, right?

You might say something like, "OK, tell me what happened (we all have a little curiosity streak in us) … I am sure it was just an honest mistake. Trust me, it's not as bad as it seems. You know you are amazing!!! You are smart, talented, and they hired an incredible person for the job. C'mon, shake it off … it will be better tomorrow."

Or you might take the approach to help your friend use the perceived mistake as an opportunity instead, "Just think, you can always use this as an opportunity to learn. What would you do differently if given the chance, or if the same situation happened?"

Either way, you can imagine a dialogue about something of this nature to make my point. If a friend or colleague calls you about a bad day they are having, or a mistake they made, you would be very considerate and purposeful about finding the right words to help lift them back up, to soothe them, to give them permission to fail. But what about when it's *you* that had the bad day?

How are you talking to yourself when you make a mistake, or things don't go your way? Likely, the dialogue goes a little more like this: "UGH, today sucks!!! I totally screwed up majorly and I am so stupid! I have no idea why they hired me, I can't do anything right! I am such a loser, I really an am idiot. Why do I even bother, I know I am just going to get fired anyways … blah, blah, blah."

And, so on and so on …

You get the point, right? Not only do you exhibit no patience for yourself or the mistake you made, you also berate yourself in the worst way possible. You continue to beat yourself up to the point of exhaustion and pure disgust. You will proceed to ruin the rest of your day, demean your own self-worth, make bad choices (e.g., drink or eat or medicate your troubles away, decide not to exercise, or just crawl into bed defeated), and resolve to let one small instance affect a chain of events to follow as a result.

And if that wasn't enough torture to your mind, your heart, and your sense of self, you will wake up the next morning feeling like a failure and already start your day on the wrong foot. You will begin to perpetuate more "screwups" and begin to create a vicious circle for yourself. This negative self-talk could destroy not only the rest of your day that day the incident happens, but your entire week, or, worse, it could even create a much longer-lasting debilitating effect on your life, your job, your relationships, and how you generally perceive yourself.

Whew, I am exhausted just thinking about all that negativity! Now, I am exaggerating a bit here (but then again, maybe I am not), but, you do see my point! If you begin to layer that moment of negativity and self-loathing with another moment where you are tearing yourself down, with yet another moment, and another moment after that, you can see how this can create a very negative and powerful domino effect.

You get to a point where you actually start to believe those words deep inside you. Consciously, you say them, and unconsciously, you hold them heavy in your heart and mind. Yet, you would *NEVER* use those words, that language, or that negativity to a friend, or even with a stranger. You would be appalled if you heard someone else talk so maliciously and hatefully to another. But yet, you do it to yourself *ALL* the time!

We don't generally stop to be purposeful in our own internal dialogue. We speak from a place of reaction, versus giving the situation time to breathe, space to unfold itself, while trying our best to remain practical and realistic in what actually transpired. Just think for a moment what might happen if you talked to yourself differently.

Let me give you another example. This one regards our attempt to "lose" weight, as this is a common issue many of us face. At one point in our lives, most of us have attempted some sort of diet or two. So, let's talk about why you might not be as successful as you would like when it comes to weight management or living a healthier lifestyle.

Have you ever thought it might be the words you choose to talk to yourself as you are going through the process? The way you design your own self-talk? How what you say and think might be holding you back, or sabotaging your efforts, and you didn't even realize it?

OK, let's play this out a couple of different ways:

Original Self-Talk:
Your internal dialogue or the words you speak to others might go something like this: "I am so fat, I am disgusting. I never seem to be able to stay on track. It's so hard for me, I don't know how to eat healthy. I hate working out"

Sound familiar? Well, think about the words and phrases you are using. All of these are negative. By focusing on what we don't want, we are creating just that. Our minds don't differentiate words like "don't" as much as they do on the *what* we actually are talking and thinking about. By saying, "I don't want to be fat," your mind says, "Fat … OK, I need to be fat." What if, instead of focusing on the negative of your current state, you start to focus, rather, on your desired state?

Let's change our language to reflect a more purposeful and intentional focus:

Revised Self-Talk:
"I choose to be healthy. I know I am in control to make the changes I want to see. I am strong and capable. My workouts are a way to achieve greater success. I fuel myself with good food in order to maximize my results, get fit, and begin to live a healthier lifestyle. I am capable of making my own change happen."

See the difference? Pay attention to how your own body language may have changed as a result of using more uplifting and empowering words. Did your visual images change? How do you feel?

Let's try another example:

Original Self-Talk:
You make a proud statement to yourself and others when you drop a few pounds … "I lost ten pounds."

That should feel great, right? That's what you were trying to accomplish all along, isn't it? So, then, why am I using that as an example? Think about the word "lost" for a moment and how your mind reacts to it. Your brain isn't thinking about the ten pounds but instead the strong action verb you used. What do I mean by that? Think about every other way your brain frames the word "lost" in conversation with such statements like: "I lost my keys, I lost my iPhone, I lost my job, I lost my dog."

How do your mind and body react when you sense or know something is *lost*? You feel tense and anxious, because now you want to find something, right? "Lost" implies something was taken from you, or it was out of your control, or you need to get back something. You want to find those keys or your cell phone, or get a new job, or find your lost puppy, right?

So, why wouldn't you want to find those pounds again, too? Hmmm, interesting perspective. So, what might be a better way to express the same thing, yet with a very different physiological response? Instead, what if we tried something like this:

Revised Self-Talk:
"I released ten pounds" or "I gave away ten pounds"

Feels better, doesn't it. Did you notice how your mind and body responded to the new phrase? Did you let out a sigh of relief and feel your body relax more? Why do you think that is?

Well, "released" or "gave away" implies a choice, that you have control over the outcome. You made the decision to let go of something that is no longer needed. For all you know, those ten pounds might serve someone else, like an underprivileged child, more (OK, slight exaggeration, but again, I'm trying to illustrate a point). But by your giving it away freely, and allowing yourself control of the outcome, you know that you are safe in letting it go. It is there for someone else to have, whoever needs it more versus keeping it for yourself. You no longer are fighting with yourself, even if only sub-consciously, to get it back.

Just two simple examples of how words have tremendous power. The more we can be intentional and purposeful about which words we choose, and how and when we use them, the more we start to control our responses to outside stimuli.

We all struggle with our own internal dialogue from time to time, even when we try to be intentional. We learn behaviors and create responses by watching how others in our immediate circle react, by receiving feedback from others, or by protecting ourselves from experiences we personally have had, or simply in trying to keep ourselves safe. These learned behaviors often become automatic responses.

It was ironic, as I was preparing to give a talk on this particular subject a while back, I was going through a personal life change of my own. I had decided to leave my corporate security blanket to venture out on my own as a coach and consultant. I decided to move cross-country and start my own business.

As I was experiencing the new decision and change going on in my life, I had a friend ask me one day how I was feeling about all the transitions. My immediate response was, "I am so overwhelmed with how many people have reached out to me, are supportive of me, and all the love I am receiving."

Not two seconds after I said the words, I stopped myself and thought about what I had just said. The word "overwhelming" felt extremely heavy and it took me only a few seconds to realize why.

So, I quickly interjected, "Wait, that's not right. I am not feeling overwhelmed in any way. Overwhelmed is such a heavy and anchoring word, and everything I am feeling is the exact opposite of that. I feel very light and uplifted. I am not feeling overwhelmed at all, but rather (and I was trying to be much more purposeful in finding the accurate way to describe how I was feeling) ... I am overflowing with gratitude for all the love, support, and outreach I'm receiving from my network. It is wonderful and I feel truly blessed."

Wow, my body language changed instantly! I released a huge audible sigh and felt extremely light and relaxed. My smile got bigger and I truly felt the words I chose to say versus the ones that flew out of my mouth before that without me thinking first (bad habits are hard to break, for me, too). And now I keep telling myself how much I am overflowing with gratitude.

Even when the beginnings of fear or doubt crept in (trust me, it's human nature, no matter how intentional you are, to have these feelings show up from time to time), I do my best to refocus and choose my words more carefully. For I now recognize just how much power words can have when I use them to others and for myself.

Speaking of fear, I also am grateful to have some of it present itself every now and again, as it makes me more centered and grounded in what I truly want to accomplish. Healthy fear keeps me focused and more purposeful in the direction I am going. As soon as I recognize it, I acknowledge it (make sure there is not something I need to adjust or tend to) and then I release it.

I remind myself of all the things I have accomplished and how I am capable of so much more. I know I am exactly where I am supposed to be and on the path I am destined to travel. I realize that the journey is the blessing and I am loving the ride, all of it.

Remember, where there is a will … YOU are the way! And fear is simply the lies we continue to tell ourselves.

By becoming more intentional and purposeful about the words you choose, you also change your actions as a result. When we tell ourselves, "I will" or "I am" or "I have" versus "I might" or "I wish" or "I hope," we change the focus and our activity to *make* things happen. The prior options indicate something has already been accomplished; you are living presently in the desired state. The latter allows room for doubt. You may or may not accomplish something, and much of the outcome is dictated by outside factors and influences, versus you being the driver of your own desires.

Don't forgot: You are responsible, and you have the power to decide. You become what you give the most energy to, so put your energy in the thoughts that serve you best.

Fear and doubt do not have an active role in decided statements, such as "I will," "I am," and "I have." These are powerful frames you establish for yourself. Think about anything you have known would happen; there was no doubt, so it did. You used powerful statements and thoughts to make that true. "I will be a top sales producer," "I will move to a new city," "I will run that race" ... And you did, just by saying and thinking it so. And you *did* because you created intentional actions to make those statements a reality.

So, it is up to you to let go of the fear, the doubt, and the negativity in the words and thoughts you choose. Change your frames and be intentional about the words you use for yourself as much as with others. Allow your mind to embrace all the greatness that you are and can be! Another way we are going to discuss being more intentional is to stop "should-ing" all over yourself ...

"Whether you think you can or you think you can't, you're right."
– Henry Ford

Call to Action

1) Assess your own self-talk and ask yourself, "Am I being intentional about the words I use with myself and thoughts I have about myself?" Pay attention to your own body language with your own self-talk. Do you notice any patterns or words that are extremely negative or heavy anchors?

2) Identify those negative and anchoring words you use regularly to evaluate your performance, your thoughts, your ideas, your dreams. Are you sabotaging what you want by the words you choose? What are the words that seem to repeat themselves over and over in your self-talk?

3) Once you identify the words that are anchoring you, or limiting you in your current beliefs, determine the words that represent an opposite frame that drives toward your desired outcome. Change your frame and words to represent a positive and uplifting outlook (e.g., turn a statement such as, "I am always late to everything" to a more positive action and choice-based statement, "I will learn to prioritize my time to allow me to become more punctual"). Remember, you become that which you give the most energy and thought to.

4) Vow today to become more intentional about the words you choose for yourself. Are you really feeling "overwhelmed" or are you overflowing with gratitude? One statement holds onto the negative, while the other allows you to feel lighter, more abundant.

5) Create a personal mantra (e.g., "where there's a will …") or positive affirmations for yourself that you repeat daily. Find a place where you are able to quiet down your own mind to do this—before you go to sleep at night, first thing in the morning, in your car, when you are cooking, etc. This can be something you just think to yourself, though stating it out loud for your own ears to hear creates an even more powerful influence on your subconscious and internal self-talk.

6) For greater personal accountability, take your affirmations a step further. Write them down and post them where you will see them most: on your mirror in the bathroom, in your car, in your wallet. Record them so you can listen to them as you fall asleep at night, or when you wake up first thing in the morning before doing anything else, or when you are by yourself, or during meditation.

7) Tell a trusted friend that you are trying to be more intentional about your own self-talk and ask the friend to help hold you accountable when and if he or she hears you use limiting and anchoring negative words with yourself so you can stay fully present and create greater awareness to become more intentional.

six

Destroy the Noise: Stop 'Should-ing' All Over Yourself

"Your time is limited, so don't waste it living someone else's life."
– Steve Jobs

"I should go to college and get *that* degree. I should apply for *that* job. I should date or marry *that* man. I should start having kids now. I should look like everyone else. I should be strong and not so emotional. I should know better. I should settle down. I should act my age and stop dreaming so much. I should play small. I should … I should … I should … I should …"

Good grief! How many times do we "should" on ourselves in one day? Who else do we let "should" all over us? Our parents, our in-laws, our friends, our teachers, our mentors, our colleagues, our bosses, our church, and even our society? Everywhere around us, we are being "should-ed," and oftentimes, we don't even realize it.

Norms, traditions, culture, upbringing, environment, circumstances, the past, the future, the present, fear, insecurities … just to name a few, all play into our psyche and influence the way we think and what we think we "should" do, say, think, and believe. And all those "shoulds" from everyone else are a result of their current think-ing, past experiences, their own insecurities, fear, and inability to break free from their own barriers being projected at us. Yet, we take all of that and internalize it as our own truth.

Again, no wonder you feel exhausted, or defeated, or like you really don't know which way is up. You are so busy taking on every-one else's "shoulds" in addition to your own, making them your truth and your reality. It doesn't have to be this way.

For instance, if your mother tells you that you "should" do some-thing, know that this is coming from her view of the world as she sees it right in that particular moment. It is limited in whatever chains she has shackled around herself, whatever filters she uses to interpret her own truths, and whatever fears she allows to control her sense of self-worth. It also could be a function of her having a bad day or being distracted and not fully present in what she is saying to you.

Regardless, she doesn't do this intentionally as a means of ill intent (usually), or to shut you down in most cases (though that could be a possibility sometimes, too). She does it more from a place of comfort, fear, and repetition, and truly from her perspective and what she knows. She could be afraid, or stuck, or she hasn't learned the tools to think outside her own comfort zone, so she projects all this to you as a means to simply try to protect you and keep you safe. And because *your* mother "told you so," you take this on as your personal truth, as well.

When, in fact, the only truth is the decision you make on how you choose to interpret what you think and hear. The only truth is the per-spective you provide yourself. If you think you cannot do something, that becomes your truth. If you think you can, the same principle applies. If you think you "should" do something, that will become your truth, too, until or unless you choose another truth. In order to find a new truth, you must change your current perspective.

A few years back, one of my best friends from high school said to me, after a recent breakup I had just gotten out of, that I "should really dial it down." To say I was caught a little off guard is an understatement, as this was someone in my innermost circle of friends and who I thought accepted me for *me*. I took about half a second to respond back, and ask, "Dial down what? The core essence of who I am and what I represent? Dial down *me* and the fact that I choose not to be like everyone else?"

She then responded, "Well, I am just saying that if you want to meet someone, you are going to have to dial it down. You can be really intense and over-the-top sometimes."

"Wow, I see," I said, a bit stunned and with great clarity. "I am not willing to dial *anything* down, as I love that I stand on my own, and I know who I am, and that I choose to travel a different road than most. There are people who purposely seek me out as a result of *who* I am and want to be around me because of my passion, my intensity, and because I don't play small or pretend to be anyone other than who I am. As much as it would pain me to see you leave, *you* really do have a choice to walk away if you truly think I am *too* much."

And, sadly, so she did just that. Don't get me wrong, I do miss my friend and what we shared for over twenty years, but I also recognize that we were growing apart and my playing as big as I did was not comfortable for her. So, I let her go and we ended our friendship as a result. I made a responsible decision to not allow her "should-ing" to stand in the way of my authenticity.

You see, I am very clear in who I am and what sets me apart. I also acknowledge and have made peace with the fact that I am not for everyone. And for those who choose to be in my light, I welcome them with open arms and an open heart. I want to surround myself with people who help me grow and continue to challenge me, those who see and appreciate me for *me*.

As I've grown in my own sense of identity over the years, I have learned that others has their own limitations on what is comfortable and acceptable for them (myself included, and it is something I continually strive to have awareness about and challenge myself to grow further in). There are so many factors that play into one's perspective and how we view the world. I continue to work on not judging the choices others make, but to focus on how I can be the best version of me at all times.

And out of all these factors that affect our ability to choose, the number one thing I have found that gets in our way is fear. Fear truly is nothing more than the lies we tell ourselves as a derivative of all the "shoulds" we surround ourselves with. Many times this fear comes from instances where our own internal mirror is being held up and we don't like what we see projected back.

Rather than deal with what we don't like about ourselves or the truth we see reflected back, we find we need to project outward and attack others who may have traits that resemble ours. The idea of the "pot calling the kettle black" greatly applies here.

Though I have a friend who says it even better, "If you spot it, you got it!" I think this sums it up pretty well. Think about that. Most of the time when people lash out at you, attack you, or call you out about something, it really has nothing to do with you at all. They are feeling vulnerable or insecure about something within themselves, and instead of dealing with their perceived issues, they find someone else to pick on.

These projections then become fuel for their fire and one in which they need a reaction, any reaction, to feel justified, more in control, and validated in that particular moment. The best reaction you can have in those situations is no reaction at all.

You will find that when people are provoking you—and remember they are doing so for their own personal agenda and insecurities (this is *not* about you at all)—they won't know what to do if you don't participate in their game. No reaction serves as a means to shut them down immediately and allows you to make a conscious choice to *not* internalize their drama, or their fear.

Let me give you a real example I experienced one night when I was out with a group of girlfriends. We were out at a fabulous martini piano bar having a great time, when this gentleman tapped me on the shoulder. I turned around, and I could instantly tell he was in a foul mood and looking to start a heated debate. Immediately, he confirmed my initial assessment and said, "I don't like that jacket you are wearing." I simply shrugged, turned around, and continued talking with my friends.

A few seconds later, he tapped me on the shoulder again (a little more emphatically this time, I might add), "I don't think you heard me," he started, "I really don't like the jacket you are wearing … it's too bright and crazy." Again, I simply smiled, shrugged, and turned my attention back to my friends.

Now, the man was furious and tapped my shoulder once more, impatiently. His voice got more stern and much louder, and he repeated, "I really *do not* like your jacket!" This time, I gave him my biggest smile, paused, and replied back, "I'm sorry, but you act as if your opinion of my jacket is going to change the fact that I am having a fabulous evening out with my girls, or that I even care about your opinion of me or my jacket, in the first place. If it bothers *you* that much, *you* have a choice to walk away."

Stunned and clearly irritated, the man stormed off in a huff, and my friends all stared at me incredulously, then started to giggle. One of my girlfriends said, with some level of disbelief, "Wow, did he really think you were going to take your jacket off simply because *he* didn't like it?"

I chuckled at her very serious, yet obvious question. Then, I smiled and answered, "Yes, I think he did."

'Wow, you have to be kidding!" she then exclaimed.

"Really, why are you so surprised?" I asked. "Yes, this was a very blatant and obvious situation, but I wonder, how many of you 'take off your jacket' every day because someone tells you they don't like it?"

Silence. My friends seemed shocked and a bit baffled at my question. They all started to look around not wanting to really own up to that one.

"Well, I would never …," replied one of them.

"Really?" I inquired. "I can think of several examples where you have 'taken off your jacket' because of someone else's comments. For starters, let's look at a former employee of mine who decided to start growing out a beard," I started. "Personally, I thought it looked great on him, but his new manager made a comment to him one day as they passed each other in the hall, 'So, did we lose our razor?' she asked. The next day, he came to work completely clean-shaven. He 'took off the jacket'."

"Here's another example, I had an administrative assistant come into my office one day, almost in tears and quite upset. When I asked what was wrong, she blurted out that someone had called her a name that attacked her character. It was very apparent that this comment had completely derailed her, sucker punched her self-image, and caused her self-esteem to vanish.

I chose to bring a little perspective to the situation, and asked her how many people she knew in the organization. I mean, she had been there almost twenty years, so I was guessing it was fair to assume she knew at least two hundred people in the company. She agreed and said that was a fair statement.

I then asked her, of the two hundred people she knew (not including the person who verbally attacked her), how many would say the same thing about her. She paused and thought about it for a minute, then quietly responded that it was unlikely that anyone else would make the same comment or think that about her.

I smiled, and asked then if she was willing to allow one person, who appeared to be having a bad day and needed to lash out at someone that the attacker perceived would react, to ruin her entire day when she just told me that no one else would confirm that statement. She laughed at how insignificant it seemed from that perspective and went back to her day. Had we not discussed it, though, she would have "taken off the jacket" and let it affect at least the rest of her day, if not longer.

Think about it: if someone were to make the same comment at work to you, in the same manner as the guy at the bar, how many of you would go back to your desk, take off the jacket, and put on the safe, conservative, black sweater hanging on the back of your chair instead?

You see, you take off the jacket all the time! You constantly allow others' perceptions, judgments, and "truths" to dictate how you feel about yourself. We all do it. We look in the mirror with our favorite, colorful, crazy jacket that is full of personality and represents our own individuality and creativity, and we feel confident, proud, and able to take on the world. We take off with our head held high, confident in who we are and how we look.

Then, in one instant, when someone else questions our choice or makes a rude comment, or laughs at us, we immediately take the jacket off. The same one that a few mere hours before (or even minutes) gave us our own sense of having superpowers. We let others destroy how we value our own self-worth *all* the time. Eventually, that jacket ends up at Goodwill, or worse, thrown away, and our superpower is lost forever and a little sense of self slips away.

I urge you to stop the noise!!! Stop "should-ing" all over yourself and recognize your truths as your own. Decide what is your truth and fight for it! Stop letting others "should" all over you. Stand strong, be empowered. Wear that jacket, with all its superpowers, with confidence, and with your head held high. Be a role model and leader in stepping out of your own fear and limitations and pushing past the boundaries of your own comfort zone. Dare to be bold! Dare to be an individual!

Remember, other people's words, actions, and thoughts are not about you most of the time. Choose wisely what you will allow in to create your truths. Go back to Goodwill, or pull that jacket out of the closet or trunk you buried it in, and put it back on with pride, with confidence. The only accessory you need to add is your biggest smile to go with it!!! Wear your true colors with purpose and pride, as now is the time to put your best foot forward, set the example for what is possible, and walk the talk.

"If you hear a voice within you say 'you cannot paint,' then by all means paint and that voice will be silenced."
– Vincent Van Gogh

Call to Action

1) Acknowledge all the "shoulds" you internalize on a daily basis, from yourself and from others. Recognize that those "shoulds" and projections from others are not about you at all, and they stem from others' own limited thinking, current perspective, judgments, biases, and fear.

2) Change your perspective today. Ask these questions: "Is this my truth? Am I letting fear dictate my truths? Am I able to stretch myself and think beyond my own limitations? Do I want to?"

3) Ask yourself the questions, "Will this even matter five years from now? A week from now? Is this even about me?"

4) In any given situation where someone says something hurtful, or criticizes you, or gives you unsolicited feedback, ask, "What was my role in this situation? What am I responsible for? How do I choose to react?"

5) Understand who you are and how you want to represent yourself. Dig that favorite jacket back out of your closet or go buy a new one, and wear it, and your true colors, with purpose and pride, and let your superpowers thrive.

6) Dare to be bold and unique, and the conductor of your own orchestra! Know who you are and present that to the world with pride and conviction.

seven

Walk the Talk

*"I am not a product of my circumstances.
I am a product of my decisions."*
- Stephen Covey

How well do you really "walk the talk?" Do your actions reflect the person you want to be? Do they represent an accurate reflection of what you say and what's in your heart?

I think, in all my experience over the years working with others and holding the mirror up to myself, I find this to be the most challenging and contradictory space where people get stuck. What they say and what they do are not always aligned. So many of us have tremendous incongruence between our goals, our desires, and the actions we take.

I remember vividly a pivotal moment in my life where I was reminded of how loudly actions speak in a really big way. I had just learned some unfortunate and disheartening news about a former mentor of mine—remember, it is sometimes from our darkest hours that we find our greatest lessons. But my mentor had been arrested for what appeared to be his third drinking-under-the-influence offense. Additionally, he was charged with reckless endangerment. Fortunately, no one, other than two guardrails he hit, was injured or killed. But the impact still was felt by friends, family, and the community in which he was seen as a prominent leader, mentor, friend, and supporter.

You see, for me, the impact was profound, as he was my mentor all throughout college, one of my rocks when I was a student, when I went through some of the most difficult periods in my past, when I was the alumni president of my alma mater, and has been a mentor to me since over the years. In the moment I received the news, I felt as if I had just walked straight into a solid, brick wall and someone had punched me right in the stomach at the same time.

You may ask how I chose to deal with this situation. At first, I reacted, and wanted justification. I was hurt, angry, and in a state of disbelief. In that moment, I gave myself permission to grieve and acknowledge the emotions and thoughts I was dealing with. I was completely selfish and made the situation all about me.

Through my own barriers, I had a friend remind me that the situation was not about me at all. We all fall and fail in our lives. And this was a moment where my mentor had done just that. His mistake came with grave consequences, but still he had simply fallen. None of this changed, nor should it, the impact he had had on me when I needed him most.

You see, some of us choose to learn from those moments, while others choose not to take responsibility for their actions and learn from their experiences.

The part I personally found to be probably the hardest to come to terms with was that this was a repeated offense. I was disheartened to know that he didn't accept responsibility the first, or even second time, and allowed the pattern to continue. That was a difficult pill to swallow as he was an integral part in my developing my own sense of accountability and taking responsibility for my own actions.

But I also forgot for a moment to remember the power of forgiveness and the peace it can provide. Again I have to recognize that we all make mistakes, even our mentors and role models. And, in this case, his alcoholism took over and I realized that it was not mine to condone or make judgments about.

I did, however, decide to look deeper for the lesson I could take with me. For each of us has the power and opportunity to find his or her own truth in whatever curveballs life throws. As I thought about what happened, I realized that I found such contradiction between his words and his impact on me with his actions. That whole "walk the talk" saying kept swirling around in my head and my heart.

I envisioned how his current actions could erase all the impact he has had on so many over the years as they could feel violated, angry, hurt, as if he were a hypocrite (just a few of the emotions I allowed to bubble to the surface), among a host of other emotions and thoughts. I kept trying to understand "why," and I found I didn't have an answer.

And then I was given the ultimate answer—maybe it is not for me to understand. It was not my journey or cross to bear. Again, I was reminded that it was not about me at all, nor mine to lay judgment on. I did not own this in any way, other than to find my own truth and what I wanted to take forward from it with me.

My friend who provided me with such clarity and perspective was clear to state that the incident did not dismiss everything my mentor gave me and taught me over the years. It was up to me to determine my own perception of the situation. This reminder gave me strength and insight to recognize that I can choose what I want to take from this, what is my lesson. I could either continue to get bogged down in a myriad of emotions and negativity or I could pull myself back up and use this as an example of what I "walk the talk" about every day.

It was the reality punch I needed! So, I stopped crying and feeling like this was happening to me and decided, instead, to move on with the learnings from the experiences I had had with my mentor over the years that helped shape me into the person I am today. His actions recently did not and could not change the impact he has had in my life for over twenty years. He made a mistake, and unfortunately, it came with very grave and serious costs.

And the simple realization gleaned from all of this is that EVERY thought, EVERY action, EVERY decision you make HAS a consequence. And if you choose to be selfish in those thoughts, actions, and decisions, or choose not to take responsibility to get help if needed, it could cost you everything that matters most: your family, your reputation, your word, and your legacy.

You ARE accountable for *how* you choose to show up in this world, NO EXCUSES!!!! ... This is YOUR responsibility (no one else's), NOT a choice you get to opt into. For even if you "choose" not to be accountable and not show up with courage that too becomes a decision, AND you *will* have to accept the consequences that transpire as a result.

So, I challenge you to think about how you are choosing to show up *every* day, in *every* minute, with *every* person. What are you willing to hold yourself accountable to? And are you prepared for the consequences of the decisions you make. For the power lies within YOU, and only you!!!

When I think about how others experience me, the power of my words is very important to me. I choose to lead by example and truly "walk the talk" as best as I can. I choose to exemplify that "what you see is what you get" and to be a real, an authentic representation of the true me.

I think about how much I try to live my life by that motto every day. So much so that even the word I give my pup, Payton, holds tremendous value and importance to me. If I commit something to him, regardless that he is a dog, I make every effort to keep and execute on my word.

To make my point, let me share a story with you about how I saved "face" with Payton because I had made a promise to him. As

I was making the move cross-country to Austin from Milwaukee and starting my own coaching practice, several friends wanted to have a send-off to wish me well.

My one friend who knows how much Payton means to me (he *is* my baby) set up a happy hour at a place in Milwaukee that was dog-friendly. I was excited that Payton was going to get his own party and told him so every day all week long. I would say to him, "Are you excited that we are going to have a party for puppy Payton?" Every day I would count down with him.

The party was scheduled for a Thursday night. Payton was at puppy playcare that day. So, I picked him up, brought him home, and started to get ready to head out. I noticed storm clouds were starting to roll in. And while the place where we were having the happy hour was dog-friendly, that only included the outdoor patio. Again noticing the storms clouds rolling in and the fact that the sky was getting darker by the minute, I started to have second thoughts about bringing Payton with me.

Now, usually when I pick him up from playcare, he comes home exhausted and worn-out, then hits either the couch or bed, right away, and takes a nap. Not this Thursday! Payton sat eagerly, yet patiently, by the door … my dog is no dummy, he knew what I had promised him all week. The sky continued to look threatening and I started to weigh my options.

I knew Payton could be allowed only on the outdoor patio. I also knew that my baby boy is quite afraid of thunderstorms and only wants to hide when they hit. So, being the parent that I am, I decided I couldn't take Payton with me. No way was I going to put him in the car if it started raining nor was I willing to come home early from my own party to take care of him. So, I crouched down and said, "Sorry, bud … momma's not going to be able to take you with her tonight. Not this time."

I swear the look on Payton's face was heartbreaking—I never have seen my dog look so forlorn and sad. He knew I was letting him down and it broke my heart with every word I continued to utter to him, trying to appease myself and my ego. He continued to sit there with sad eyes and his head hung low, as if he had misbehaved or something. So, after a few more apologies and excuses, I left Payton sad, let down, and sitting at the top of the stairs in my entryway.

I got into my car and started to drive through rush-hour traffic to arrive on time at my party. The entire twenty minutes I sat in the car were agony. My stomach hurt; I felt as if I wanted to throw up. I kept playing the scene over and over in my mind and out loud until I started crying. Just as I was about to pull into the parking lot of the place where the party was being held, I instantly straightened up and made a crazy U-turn.

"What was I doing?" I muttered out loud. "I made a promise to my 'little boy' … and if I can't even keep a promise to Payton, who means more to me than anything in this world, what good is my word? Even if it rains, I will figure something out and will deal with that, when and if, it happens."

So, I turned my car around and again drove another twenty minutes through traffic, pulled up to my house, opened the door, and Payton was sitting there waiting for me, eager and happily wagging his tail. "OK, buddy, momma was wrong … this is *your* party and I promised you got to go with me. Are you ready?" He was excited and jumped into the car without hesitation, and off we went. I made it to my party about thirty minutes late, but everyone, especially me, was thrilled Payton was there.

He received all kinds of attention as everyone fussed over him. It definitely was *his* party! Payton was king of the world!!! It did, in fact, end up raining that evening. But my boy won the heart of everyone there, so much that even when it did start to rain and storm, they were kind enough to let us into the covered bar area outside, Payton included!

OK, so maybe that was a little bit of a silly story to illustrate my point, but you definitely see that your word is just that, your word. It does not matter who you make a promise to, whether it be another person, your dog, or even yourself. The point I am making is that how you decide to take action upon your word is what really counts. It doesn't matter who I give my word to. When I make a promise, I need to keep that promise.

You have the power to decide whether you will walk the talk and hold yourself accountable to a higher standard. By my doing so, I was able to stay authentic and congruent in who I am and it felt wonderful to do so. I challenge you to look at what you say to people, what you promise them and yourself, and then ask yourself whether you are being authentic? Are you congruent with who you are and who you want to be? Are you "walking the talk?"

> *"Happiness is not something ready-made.*
> *It comes from your own actions."*
> – Dalai Lama

Call to Action

1) Think of a time in the past six months when you made a promise to someone that you didn't keep. How did you feel? Were there any repercussions? How do you gain credibility and trust back? If you could do it all over again, what would you do differently today?

2) Think of a time in the past six months when you made a promise to yourself that you didn't keep. How did you feel? Were there any repercussions? Did you feel let down? How do you move forward? If you could do it all over again, what would you do differently today?

3) Make a promise today to start walking the talk. Become congruent in what you say you will do, and what's important to you and start taking action to make those things a reality.

4) Map out those things in your life that are top priorities and create an action plan to address each one. Identify both the consequences and rewards for accomplishing or not accomplishing those goals. Commit to following the plan you created.

eight

Be Coachable *Not* Controllable

*"The only person you are destined to become
is the person you decide to be."*
– Ralph Waldo Emerson

So, back in my corporate career, I was up for a promotion and a new job that I believed was ideal for me. I made it through the lengthy interview and assessment process to become one of the finalists in the running for the position. Several people indicated I was a top candidate and that I would be a great fit for the role. Weeks labored on, and still no word. Finally, I called the hiring manager to check the progress of things, only to be told that the company decided to go another way and that I wasn't the right person for the job.

I was a little annoyed and upset when I received the news. One, I felt I was led along being given the wrong impression of how I fared; and two, I had to be the one to reach out to the hiring manager to get word of the manager's decision versus the manager proactively calling me to tell me the verdict. It also didn't sit well with me that I made this call the Friday before a long holiday weekend. To think, had I not called, I would have still been under the impression I was seriously being considered for the position all weekend long.

Now, when I took a step back and checked my emotions around the situation, I honestly wasn't surprised. In the middle of the interview process, I was given some feedback that there were some mixed reviews when it came to me, my skills, and my ability to lead. People either were the biggest champion of me or claimed I was a liability and risk. There didn't really seem to be any middle ground between the two camps.

None of this was new to me. I have been able to recognize that sense of two camps throughout my career, especially once I moved into higher management roles. It came down to people either really liked me and my leadership style or they didn't. There weren't many people who didn't have an opinion one way or the other.

From my vantage point, I preferred that. I would rather have people make a decision and have conviction about how they perceive me or what they think of me than waffle around on not knowing or not being comfortable with making a statement either way. Now, I do believe I had far more champions than naysayers in my career, but those naysayers usually did carry an impactful voice.

So, that being said, and knowing that I had a few strong naysayers among all the champions, and after recognizing the situation and my truth in it, I reached out to the hiring manager to ask for additional feedback as to why I wasn't selected. Unfortunately, I didn't receive much of a *real* answer and got more of a side-stepping in his response instead.

As much as I knew the reason (or thought I did), I still wanted validation and justification as to why I wasn't hired. I told myself I needed to know this so I could decide what I wanted to take from the feedback, and what, if anything, I wanted to change or improve upon. I was under the premise that, without fully knowing the "why," it was difficult to make choices about the things I wished to improve or the things I was fully confident are part of who I am and are not up for compromise.

I realize now that the need for validation and justification is simply another way to transfer blame and not take responsibility. Ultimately, it is up to me and my own self-discipline to take on full responsibility and let go of the need to shift blame.

But I will get to that in a little bit. Back to the story at hand. Finally, another manager on the team reached out to me, as he wanted to share his insights and feedback.

So, we met, and he began to share his feedback and insight with me. Though I aced the assessment required to test my aptitude for the position, the hiring manager did decide, based on the mixed feedback he received, that I was not coachable. When I heard this, my immediate response was, "You mean I am not controllable." To which, the manager I was meeting with at the time chuckled.

"Good distinction," he said.

I then replied, "I am extremely coachable, and anyone that knows me knows that. I am always hungry for more. I want to grow and be better at the things I do well. I recognize my limitations, but I choose not to spend all my time trying to correct those things. I have a strong desire to play to my strengths and to my highest and best value. I would love to be coached, by someone willing to coach *me*, in how I can accomplish more of that. But I am also not willing to compromise who I am and play small, simply because my playing big scares people."

"I think it is interesting that while I have proven my capability and capacity to push our sales force to do more, change their thinking, and become more accountable in their own practices, *and* I scored extremely well on the assessment, I was not given the opportunity — when these are the very skills required to do what is needed in this position are those very things, and to push our sales force to be more accountable."

He agreed emphatically with my line of thinking and offered me the opportunity to approach him directly if another spot opened up on the team and I still was interested. He responded by saying he saw great things in me and that he was willing to take a chance and thought I could be coached well into the role.

I appreciate his faith and confidence in my abilities. However, everything does happen for a reason, and my career took a different direction as a result. Blessings and opportunities show up in many ways. As such, I ended up taking another opportunity that was presented to me shortly afterward.

Now, looking back on this moment in my career, I realize it was a huge catalyst for me to begin recognizing that I was spending too much time living out someone else's dream versus taking ownership of my own. I appreciated that conversation and have a tremendous amount of gratitude for the manager who took time out to give me honest and constructive feedback, as it was a very transparent mirror I was able to hold up and ask myself if those were things I wanted to change about myself. My answer was "no."

Even though the core of what was shared with me, I decided, were not things I wanted to change, I also was able to better appreciate and own my responsibility in the ways things played out. I did see that there were ways I could communicate differently, and more effectively, and could make some greater headway with some of my naysayers. For the last thing I wanted to do was to burn bridges with future relationships and potential opportunities.

• • •

Fast-forward to where I am now in my life, running my own business. I still look for ways to be coached and mentored every day to help me grow and continue to be challenged. I seek out others who will provide constructive and rich feedback, who will help keep me accountable to my own truths, and call me out if I am not walking the talk and being congruent between my actions and what I say.

However, there is a big difference between being coachable versus being controllable. Sacrificing your own sense of self, your strengths, and your values only fuels someone else's power and control over you. If, by not making these changes, because you feel they compromise who you truly are or who you want to become, you are limiting your ability to grow in an organization or be promoted within a company, maybe the time has come to assess whether you are in the right place. You might begin to explore whether the time has come to go and grow in a completely different direction.

Oftentimes, we think our only options are the ones in front of us. We lock ourselves down behind invisible walls and constraints, thinking our only option is to "play the game" or accept what is being asked of us. We are told, "If you want to succeed here, then you should or need to do this." You have the power to decide whether you want to accept that choice, because it truly is aligned with your goals, desires, and who you are, *or* you can decide differently. You can rewrite your script and road map at *any* time!!! The power lies within you. No one can empower you for greatness other than yourself!!

So, how do you react to the feedback you receive? What are the things about you that are sacred or truly representative of the person you are? How much do you allow others to put you in the "too" box, or limit your potential because of their own fear and limitations? Do you find yourself playing smaller so you don't rock the boat? Can you clearly define and articulate your key strengths as an individual, as a team member, as a leader? Are you being true and congruent in the authentic version of you? Why not? What holds you back?

Don't let other people's expectations or opinions stop your dreams from evolving, or stop you from doing what is in your heart to do. It takes courage and perseverance to be your authentic self. Don't let anyone rob you of the joy you deserve. You have the power to decide how you wish to live your life, and what you are willing to change about it.

Making this acknowledgement and commitment first is critical in starting this journey to achieving the dreams your heart desires most. People will criticize, will offer feedback on areas that need improvement. By knowing who you are and being confident in that knowledge, you then have the power to decide what pieces you want to accept and those to which you want to say, "Thank you, I appreciate the feedback," and walk away. The choice is *always* yours to make.

> *"There is only one way to avoid criticism: do nothing, say nothing, and be nothing."*
> – Aristotle

Call to Action

1) Identify the three to five strengths that are unique to who you are, and how you use those traits to be the best version of yourself. Ask yourself what you are willing to compromise or change about these skills, traits, or characteristics and what you are not.

2) Assess how you receive feedback from others. Do you listen to their suggestions, and then make choices for yourself? Or do you take the feedback you are given at face value and as your only truth? Are you able to find a balance in between?

3) How do you coach or provide feedback to others? Are you limited in thinking only one way, as if everything is black or white, right or wrong? Are you open to developing people based on their strengths versus trying to fit them into a mold? Do you coach individually or provide the same feedback to all?

4) Take time to truly understand who you are, what's important to you, and how you want others to perceive you (i.e., your personal brand). Step away from traditional labels (e.g., parent, boss, employee, mother, etc.) and identify the characteristics of *who* you are, the qualities that run to your core. Is what you are presenting to others congruent with how you define yourself?

nine

Go Big, or Go Bigger ... Forget Going Home

*"Go confidently in the direction of your dreams.
Live the life you have imagined."*
– Henry David Thoreau

A while back, I was sitting over breakfast with a good friend, who also happened to be my running coach at the time (as I was training for my one and only half marathon). As we were fine-tuning my training plan, I blurted out, in my excitement to get started and accomplish a long-standing goal I had had, one of my favorite expressions, "Go big, or go home, baby!"

My friend turned to me and said with genuine wonder, "Why do you say that?"

"Say what?" I asked, not sure of where he was going with his question.

"Go big, or go home ... why do you say 'go home'? Because, seriously Candy, whenever you go big, you *never* go home! It's more like you 'go big ... or go bigger'!"

Boom! I almost shot out of my seat with extreme delight, and shrieked, "I love it!!! I am so stealing that as my new saying (did I mention I like my mantras)! You are right, that is *so* me! I never go home once I commit to something, never! From now on, it's 'go big, or go bigger'!"

So, "go big, or go bigger" was born. When you make a commitment to do something, anything, give it everything you've got. Don't go halfway in, or just enough to put a toe in and test the waters, knowing that you have an out if you want it. Go all in. Take the dive!

For when you do, you are more likely to accomplish the end goal you are seeking. You become so much more intentional about going after that goal that the idea that it won't happen, or might not happen, doesn't even cross your mind.

If you are going to put any effort forth to make something happen, why wouldn't you put your heart into it as well. A half-baked effort will only yield a half-baked result. You get back what you put in. You reap what you sow.

Once you make the decision to start (and to go) in the first place, the only other option is to go even bigger. Now, if you fail, that only serves to show you what didn't work and opens up all kinds of opportunities to try other things. And, by going bigger, you will never be able to doubt or question whether failing or not accomplishing the goal was a function of your not giving it your all. You will know it is simply because you need to try a different approach instead.

I personally think the greatest regret or loss of an opportunity is to sit and wonder "what might have been" and play the "what-if" game over and over again. What if I would have tried harder? What if I would have gone all in? What if I wouldn't have been so afraid? What if I would have taken responsibility for my thoughts and actions? What if I wouldn't have 'gone home'? What if, what if, what if ...

Instead of asking every what-if in the book, I would rather use my energy to dream up what is even more possible. How can I go bigger? How can I do more? How can I impact and influence others for greatness? What would happen if I gave more, dared more, lived more? How can I play bigger, instead of smaller? How can I inspire others to do the same?

I want to spend my life *living*, truly living in every sense of the word. I want to be able to constantly take flight and soar to new heights. Like the eagle I mentioned in the beginning of this book and is illustrated on the front cover, along with all its beauty and light, I want to seek new opportunities, be free in my quest for greatness and become a visionary in what truly is possible for my future.

What about you? Do you dare to dream big and then really go after it? Will you have the courage to step up and commit fully to the goals you have for your life? Are you ready to jump in and "go big, or go bigger"? Or will you, once again, decide to "go home"? Only you can decide and the choice and power lie within you, and only you.

> *"Whatever you can do, or dream you can, begin it.*
> *Boldness has genius, power and magic in it."*
> – Johann Wolfgang von Goethe

Call to Action

1) Think about something you really wanted in your life that you only went half-way in when going after it. What were the results? What would have happened had you gone all in? Is that still something you want? Are you ready to go all in now?

2) What do you spend most of your time dreaming about? What is stopping you from making that a reality?

3) Ask yourself: What am I most afraid of when it comes to going after my goals? Is it fear of failing, fear of success, or something else? Why am I afraid of that? What would happen if I let go of my fear? What if I had conviction and knew I couldn't "go home"? Would my actions be different?

ten

Celebrate the Victories & the Failures No Matter How Small

"You miss 100% of the shots you don't take."
–Wayne Gretzky

Accountability, accountability, accountability … I cannot stress enough the need for personal accountability throughout this process and your journey. I will talk more specifically about personal accountability in just a moment, but first I want to make sure you are set up for success and we have established the right measures to gauge your progress and achievement along the way.

In order to truly accept the notion of personal accountability, we must first give ourselves the permission to *fail*. "Fail? What, are you crazy?" I am sure you are sitting there right now, feeling a bit panicked and uncertain, as you see this four-letter word jump off the page.

Right now, you might be telling yourself, "Everything I do, everything I manage, everything I have done is so that I won't fail! I have put my life in order and control things to mitigate the chance that I might fail, and now you are asking me to give myself permission to do just that? Seriously, you must be crazy!"

Yes, that is exactly what I am challenging you to do. Especially all you type A personalities and perfectionists out there, who are driven and motivated by success and accomplishments ... I *need* you, and you *need* you, to give yourself even more permission to fail (and, trust me, I say this as a recovering perfectionist myself).

I am going to help push you off the cliff of your comfort zone and teach you how to fly again. If you keep standing on the edge of the diving board, only putting a toe in to test the waters from time to time, I am going to be the one standing behind you to push you in. You *know* how to swim, so swim.

What is holding you back? We often become so afraid to fail or comfortable in our current capabilities and accomplishments that we forget to push ourselves for something more. We end up on autopilot, even if (and in many cases because of) the fact that we are top performers, excelling at what we do. It's time to stretch those wings again and remember how to fly.

Without failing, we cannot continue to grow. We hold ourselves back and find excuses when the journey gets tough, or we simply forget how to pick ourselves back up when we fall down and scrap our knees. We fear what others will say, what we will look like, that we will make a fool of ourselves, how others will judge us or laugh at us, or that we are not able to be perfect in our quest.

Again, as a recovering perfectionist, I find this thinking and fear can be so limiting, yet the very thing that stands in my way most. That and the flip side, which is the power of letting my light shine too big. It becomes a game of learning which "dog to feed'," as the one you feed is the one you give more fight and opportunity to.

But back to failing for a moment. Failing is an *opportunity* to try something else, something different, something new. The idea that we continue to do the same thing over and over again expecting different results is the clear definition of insanity. And those of us who have been very successful in our lives and career know this, acknowledge this intellectually. Yet, when push comes to shove, we get in our own way time and time again. We don't practice what is preached to us, and what we preach to others. We are not walking the talk.

The only way to test, stretch, and fine-tune our skills is to fail. We will never know or be able to expand our limitations and horizons otherwise. Seek out opportunities (and, yes, create a mind-set that allows you to see failing as opportunity, a learning mechanism, a gift for what is further possible) to fail. Embrace the process of falling and being able to pick yourself back up. You will find that you grow stronger with each fall. Now that you are failing, let's celebrate!

"What? Now I am certain that you are crazy! You want me to celebrate failing?" many of you likely are muttering or exclaiming to yourself, appalled that I would even suggest such a thing. "First, you ask me to give myself permission to fail, then you want me to celebrate failing! Who is crazy enough to celebrate failing?"

You are. If you want to create a sustainable way for you to continue to grow and achieve more, then it is imperative that you celebrate the milestones along the way. Whenever you hit a roadblock and stumble, celebrate that you gave yourself the permission to fall. Then celebrate when you pick yourself up and find a new way to move forward. Take time to assess the learning throughout the process of failing. I read somewhere that "the greatest gift is in the journey itself. Never ever return a gift to God that has been unopened or unappreciated." Recognize and celebrate *all* the gifts along the way.

And the celebrations don't always have to be big, monumental things. It can simply be that you give yourself praise, or pat yourself on the back. Or, after you hit so many milestones, determine what things motivate you, and treat yourself to something (a new experience, a new toy, etc.). Just be careful not to reward yourself with the very thing getting in your way (e.g., you reward yourself with food when emotional eating is one of your barriers). Find another motivator, but make sure you have motivators.

Enlist others for help and support you along your journey. Personal accountability is much easier when we make commitments to others and are visible with our purpose and intention. The more front and center you become about the goals you are trying to take on, the more you can rally those who support you most when you find yourself hitting a wall, or fearing creeping back in, or when you are simply "stuck" once more.

Identify your true champions and advocates, who see you as you are now and support you in who you are trying to become. You have no time for the doubters, the naysayers, or any toxic energy if you are to achieve great things. Instead, surround yourself with love, support, encouragement, and belief in you.

Personal accountability is the key to creating long-term, sustainable change and the lifestyle you envision. As I mentioned a few times in this book, "where there's a will, there is a YOU." For it is up to YOU, and you alone, to make the conscious decision and effort to achieve the greatness you so desire. No one else will get it done for you, and even if someone did, it would not be far as rewarding.

This is *your* script, *your* dreams, *your* life. There will be noise coming at you from all directions, in the form of "shoulds" and "should nots," those who think you are crazy, limiting beliefs (your own and from others), fear, your daily routine, laziness … and the list goes on and on.

The more you can be present and personally accountable to making the changes you want in your life, the more you will be able to quiet, and eventually eliminate, the noise around you and inside you altogether. It takes self-discipline, vision, and perseverance. Like any new learned behavior or habit, the only way to make it stick is through practice. You learned the behaviors you have now; you can learn these new strategies as well.

"I've missed more than 9,000 shots in my career. I've lost almost 300 games. 26 times I've been trusted to take the game-winning shot and missed. I've failed over and over and over again in my life. And that is why I succeed."
–Michael Jordan

Call to Action

1) Identify areas in your life where you can stretch yourself to the point of failure. Then give yourself permission right now that you are allowed to fail. In fact, you want to fail. You want to learn how to fall down and pick yourself back up again.

2) Celebrate the milestones and reward yourself for progress, any progress, including your failures. Congratulate yourself for stretching and for allowing yourself to fall.

3) Take opportunity to reflect and learn from each failure. Use this as a catalyst to try new things and think differently.

4) Identify any patterns that emerge and start to repeat them. Understand where your fear is stemming from, and why? Decide today to be purposeful and try something else, something far out of your comfort zone.

5) Create a personal accountability system to help you walk the talk. Enlist the support of your champions and advocates to help you create opportunities and sustainability.

6) Practice, practice, practice. Give yourself time to learn a new behavior and a different way of thinking. Remember, repetition is the key.

eleven

The 3 'Is: Inspire, Influence, Impact

"Strive not to be a success, but rather to be of value."
–Albert Einstein

People are attracted to attraction power. You influence and impact people every day without even knowing it. There are people that look to you for guidance, for support, or to be an example for them. You create momentum just by breathing in and out every day. So, why not be more intentional and inspirational in that reality?

You can be the example of what you want others to follow, what greatness you want others to see and live their life in accordance with. You can pay it forward. You can be more courageous and purposeful about the choices you make and what you are setting forth for yourself and for others. You can walk the talk, live large, and show your truths.

We tend to be a very self-sacrificing culture, where we extend ourselves so much for the care and benefit of others (whether it be our kids, our family, our friends, our jobs, etc.). First, realize it is not up to you to take on the struggles of the entire world. You do not need to become a martyr for everyone else's troubles, insecurities, and lives.

Second, in order to be *everything* you can and want to be for everyone else, it first comes with taking care of and being purposeful in the things you do for yourself. You must live your life first, feed that life, before you can give to others. You can only give that which you have to give and have replenished. And if you aren't 100 percent yourself, you cannot possibly give anything close to that to others.

Nurturing others starts with nurturing yourself. In order to nurture yourself, you must practice humility with dignity. Learn how to be selfless while giving self-care to yourself. The foundation for your authentic self must be built and maintained in order to build the various levels of your house. Make a commitment to yourself that you will never give out what you won't or can't replenish.

Think of your energy as a personal bank account of emotion, passion, and the ability to give. You can only withdrawal what is in the account. If you don't make deposits to keep the account full, you will reach a point where you have become overdrawn, and your account will be forfeited.

Oftentimes, I work with clients who really struggle with the idea of taking care of themselves first, or getting what they need before attending to the needs of their company or of their family. This is such a difficult leap for them to make, in addition to trying to change their filters, and release other barriers getting in their way. Sometimes just changing the frame in which you think about things can really help.

For instance, I had a client tell me she really wanted to go back to school and finish her degree. She was in her early forties and had two children. She had made a decision after the first child was born to leave the job she had at that time and become a full-time mother. She loved the time she spent with her girls, yet she still felt a sense of restlessness and a desire for something more.

The more she verbalized this desire, the more she felt guilty and like she was being a bad mother for wanting to be so "selfish." We worked on why she felt this way in wanting to better herself. She claimed, "It will take time away from my girls. They need me. It is unfair for me to be gone from them like that just to pursue a degree."

So, I changed the way I framed my questions with her, in order to help her think differently about the situation. I asked, "What would you say if one of your daughters comes to you when she is forty, and she tells you she wants to go back to school to finish her degree? What options would you want her to have? How would you want her to feel about making that decision? Is it important for you that your daughters feel empowered to do more, be more, and succeed on their own terms?"

She hesitated, then replied, "Of course! I want my daughters to do anything their hearts desire. I never want them to feel limited or held back. They can be and do anything they want. And I want so much more for them. I want them to grow up to be strong, fearless women, to feel empowered and know who they are. I don't want them to grow up and ever feel like they have to make excuses for that."

"I see," I replied, "So, who do you think is their biggest role model for how they will learn to do just that? Who is teaching them to be strong, to feel empowered and to become fully aware of who they are, with no need to make apologies or excuses?"

"Oh," the words hit her square and she caught her breath. "I never thought about it that way. I guess that is me. I want to be that role model for them."

"And, you are. Whether or not you want to be, you *are* their biggest influence. They are watching you every day, and every decision you make. They watched how you talk to yourself, and what permission you give yourself to do new things. What you choose to do with that responsibility is up to you. So, what legacy do you want to leave your girls? What do you want to teach them? What do you want to show them is possible?"

A week later, she submitted her application to college and was accepted. She now is showing her daughters that they too can be anything they want. And even though she has a role of being their mom, she also is an independent, strong, confident woman who is taking the time and effort to continue to grow and improve herself. I'd say that is a pretty significant and impactful legacy she is leaving, wouldn't you?

I tell clients all the time, "If you can't do it for yourself, think about the impression and legacy you are leaving to those you care most about, your family, your children, or grandchildren, those you mentor, your team, or anyone else you want to influence."

You see, making a difference is the summation of purpose, passion, and pride. Purpose being what drives you. Passion being what fuels you. And pride being what defines you. If you say, "What difference does it make?" you are wasting the opportunity, the responsibility, and the magnitude of impact that is yours to make. You make a difference, even if you chose to opt out, that sets an example, too. What you want the message and the legacy to be is up to you.

Think about the people in your life who have made a difference to you, whom you have wanted to emulate? Why do they inspire you? What did you learn from them? How might you pay those lessons forward?

Now, think about your own legacy, what mark do you want to impress upon the people in your life, in your community, in the world? For every thought and action has a domino or ripple effect in the universe. What you put out now *will* impact and influence others later. Do you want to inspire that result or simply let the opportunity to shine your light pass you and others by?

You *do* make a difference and have a choice in what that difference could be. Choose to inspire, influence, and impact others for greatness!

"I've learned that people will forget what you said, people will forget what you did, but people will never forget how you made them feel."
– Maya Angelou

Call to Action

1) Take time to think about your legacy. What difference or impact do you want to have on those you care about? What things do you want to teach or show others?

2) Identify something you really want to do, but feel it would be selfish to pursue. Ask yourself whether depriving yourself of that desire is keeping your bank account from being full. Is this a deposit or a withdrawal? Are you taking the time to replenish what you are taking out?

3) Ask yourself: How are my choices impacting those around me? Am I setting the right example? Am I being congruent in who I am and my own legacy?

4) Decide if you still are unable to do something for yourself, can you do it for the best interest and what you want to model for those you love?

twelve

You ARE Empowered Strong!

"Whatever the mind of man can con-
ceive and believe, it can achieve."
– Napoleon Hill

Now that you have gone through principles laid out for you in this book, here's the best part—you already *are* empowered strong. Everything I shared with you, you already know. You possess the tools and skills within yourself *now*. I just helped bring them to your attention, to help you organize them in a way that allows you to be more intentional, to think differently and purposefully, and to take action immediately to be and achieve so much more.

Think about all the accomplishments in your life to date. Identify all the times where you succeeded when you put your mind and heart to the goal. You have done this many times in your life before. Again, you *are*, and always have been, empowered strong! I have not given you any tools you didn't already possess before we started this journey. I simply gave you the keys to unlock that potential, and a mirror to realize your own capacity for greatness. A means to help you get "unstuck" and set yourself and your song free.

Regardless of having the tools and skills needed, it still is up to you to decide whether to accept the challenge, tap into your potential, and truly live your life large, out loud, and empowered strong. I hope you will embrace your talent, your uniqueness, and your ability to shine a light that is only yours. The world awaits your song, and I hope you have the courage to sing it from your heart and as your beautiful, authentic self.

I leave you with this last thought to help you stand strong and to let you know what you can accomplish each and every day:

I Am Empowered Strong

I have a song in my heart that makes me feel alive.
It is up to me to share that song with the world.
I have a unique harmony.
I let it resonate from the depths of my soul.
I am calm in my everyday tasks.
I have peace around my life decisions.
I am gentler and kinder to others, including myself.
I speak from my heart and not from behind my barriers.
I appreciate the beauty around me and within me.
I have the keys and the power to free my soul.
I am centered and focused on what truly matters most.
I live my life to the fullest in every moment.
I am becoming the best version of myself every day.
I know and respect that this is a work-in-progress.
I love completely and without restraint.
I love myself fully without judgment.
I am true to my word, my beliefs, and my values.
I am influencing greater good in the world.
I am leaving my mark and creating a legacy.
I am inspiring others to do more, love
more, give more, and be more.
I walk the path of what truly is possible.
I *am* empowered strong!

Remember, **You Empowered Strong** *can* be anything *you* dare to dream! You are the conductor for the music you wish to share, and your song is a unique gift that is yours and yours alone.

Thank you for allowing me to share in your journey. I hope you find these tools helpful in your quest to follow your dreams. Remember, the only thing holding you back right now is *you*. Release your fears, old thinking, doubt, and judgment, and give yourself permission to dream big, to fail, and to live even bigger.

For you, my friend, hold the power to be *great* within yourself. You have everything you need. Now, reach in, dig deep, and set yourself free. Go forth, be great, and shine your amazing light!!

"When I stand before God at the end of my life, I would hope that I would not have a single bit of talent left and could say, I used everything you gave me."
– Erma Bombeck

"Twenty years from now you will be more disappointed by the things that you didn't do than by the ones you did do, so throw off the bowlines, sail away from safe harbor, catch the trade winds in your sails. Explore, Dream, Discover."
–Mark Twain

About the Author

Candy Barone, the "Pull-No-Punches" Accountability Powerhouse (CCP, MBA) is a certified life strategies and accountability coach, business consultant, author, and motivational speaker, and the founder of **You Empowered Strong LLC**. She is an established professional with almost twenty years of experience coaching, executing business growth realization, strategic planning, consultative solutions, process improvement, and team development. She has held various positions with Fortune 500 companies, such as Johnson Controls and General Electric, as well as with Northwestern Mutual, Landis & Gyr, Northern Illinois Gas (NICOR), and Milwaukee School of Engineering.

After going through her own personal and professional assessment, Candy made the decision to leave the corporate world in order to give her full attention to building out her coaching and consulting practice. She moved cross-country from Milwaukee to make her dream a reality.

She is passionate about serving others and providing people with the tools they need to truly empower themselves. She has worked with experienced professionals, business owners, entrepreneurs, and leaders in helping them recognize their own potential to achieve greater success.

In addition to serving in her community (she currently volunteers her time with Dress for Success), Candy also has built and facilitated a school-to-work program, a violence-prevention program for Milwaukee Public Schools, a junior engineering program, an educational programming for youth based on science, technology, and engineering, and training programs for executives and business professionals.

Candy has a bachelor of science degree in mechanical engineering (BSME) from the Milwaukee School of Engineering, and a master of business administration (MBA) from Cardinal Stritch University. She also is a certified coach practitioner, a Law of Attraction practitioner, a Six Sigma Black Belt, and a Prosci change-management agent.

She currently lives in Austin with her dog, Payton, and enjoys all the city has to offer. She loves the outdoors, being active, and spending time with her family and friends. She is a change agent who advocates empowerment, leadership, and social responsibility.

Made in the USA
Middletown, DE
09 March 2015